HEAVEN
SIGHTINGS

Books Compiled and Written by James Stuart Bell

From Bethany House Publishers

Heaven Sightings

Life-Changing Miracles

Gifts From Heaven

Jesus Talked to Me Today

Encountering Jesus

Heaven Touching Earth

The Spiritual World of the Hobbit

Angels, Miracles, and Heavenly Encounters

From the Library of A.W. Tozer

From the Library of Charles Spurgeon

Love Is a Flame

Love Is a Verb (with Gary Chapman)

Love Is a Verb Devotional (with Gary Chapman)

HEAVEN SIGHTINGS

Angels, Miracles, and
Glimpses *of the* Afterlife

COMPILED BY
JAMES STUART BELL

BETHANYHOUSE
a division of Baker Publishing Group
Minneapolis, Minnesota

Published by Bethany House Publishers
11400 Hampshire Avenue South
Bloomington, Minnesota 55438
www.bethanyhouse.com

Bethany House Publishers is a division of
Baker Publishing Group, Grand Rapids, Michigan

Printed in the United States of America

ISBN 978-0-7642-3257-2

Library of Congress Cataloging-in-Publication Control Number: 2018053548

The following are true stories, but some details and names have been changed in order to protect privacy.

Editorial services provided by Jeanette Gardner Littleton Publication Services.

Cover design by LOOK Design Studio

19 20 21 22 23 24 25 7 6 5 4 3 2 1

In keeping with biblical principles of creation stewardship, Baker Publishing Group advocates the responsible use of our natural resources. As a member of the Green Press Initiative, our company uses recycled paper when possible. The text paper of this book is composed in part of post-consumer waste.

To Madgie B—
heaven grows ever closer to us

I saw Eternity the other night
Like a great Ring of pure and endless light,
All calm, as it was bright,
And round beneath it, Time in hours, days, years
Driv'n by the spheres
Like a vast shadow moved, In which the world
And all her train were hurl'd.

Henry Vaughan (1621–1695)
metaphysical poet
from his poem "The World"

Contents

Acknowledgments

Many thanks once again to the editorial side: David Horton, Andy McGuire, and Ellen Chalifoux, for always making my books better. And to the people I encountered in promoting *Heaven Sightings*, namely, Sheridan Nelson, Chandler Carlson, and Arielle Wade.

Introduction

How often do you think about heaven? Do you consider how all of life's problems will cease and you will enjoy intimate fellowship with God in a glorious paradise forever and ever? Perhaps those thoughts are impacted by the state of your earthly journey and your understanding of scriptural descriptions of the eternal state of bliss with the Trinity, the heavenly hosts, and the body of Christ. However, heaven is not merely a future state, but a reality that interpenetrates our own daily existence.

We need fresh eyes, inspired by the Holy Spirit, to receive glimpses of heaven in our midst. The closest example to heaven itself may be a near-death experience where some fortunate person gets a glimpse of heaven itself but then returns to his or her body and earthly existence. The perspective of anyone who has had this experience is forever changed. But there are so many other types of heavenly sightings that God makes available to us, if we have the spiritual eyes to see.

The healing of relationships, miraculous financial provision, physical healings, and close encounters with Jesus and angels in times of desperation all point to the heavenly reality in our midst, even if we only get a fleeting glimpse. These examples and many more are meant to be stimulants to our faith and comforts along life's arduous journey. We all need to pray for grace to see the miracles that we tend to either explain away or take for granted in our daily lives.

Here is a volume of testimonies to God's divine intervention where it really matters, where we need a miracle or we will fail, lose, or even die. God will come through when we need Him most. The Lord will meet you in your time of need, both in the small details and in the gravest of situations. I pray that you are inspired by the variety of God's distinct supernatural actions in each of these stories and will come to the recognition that God will use whatever means necessary to work on your behalf in all areas of your earthly life. May you have "heaven sightings" of His faithfulness and receive divine intervention constantly for your good.

James Stuart Bell

Bad Blood

Wanda J. Burnside

I loved being a primary school teacher. Each year my classroom was filled with a group of energetic first-graders. As their teacher, I had to be ready to swing into action, too.

Every day, I strived to provide interesting activities and lessons for my young students. I spent my evenings working on projects to keep those young minds thrilled about learning.

Well, that wasn't all that I had to do. I was, and am, a wife, housekeeper, Sunday school teacher, youth leader, and community worker, too. And at that time, I was very involved with the care and concerns of my aging parents.

Yet something strange was happening to me. I felt burned out so quickly. I had to press on and make myself do everything. I began to feel as if I were climbing a mountain when I walked up stairways. Walking to our car in the parking lot was like crossing a wide terrain. It took me longer and longer to do simple chores like fixing dinner, shopping, and doing housework. Teaching became more of a struggle than fun.

I never complained, but my husband, Simmie, noticed my emotions and attitudes were changing. I got the work done, but I had little energy. Simmie often said, "Wanda, stop overdoing it. You need to quit doing everything!"

"I'm not doing everything! I'll cut back," I said. But I felt tired most of the time.

Soon my mom noticed my sluggishness. I love Thanksgiving with my family and close friends. I enjoy cooking the food, decorating the house, and baking the pies; I love everything about Thanksgiving. However, that year I wasn't excited about Thanksgiving.

Happily, we had a beautiful Thanksgiving dinner with loads of food at our family gathering. I got through Thanksgiving without any weakness. I was even blessed to make it through Christmas and pressed right into the new year without any problems.

However, in early spring, I began to feel the weariness again. That was when I decided to call my doctor and make an appointment. The receptionist asked me why I needed to see the doctor; I said I felt tired all of the time.

"I see," she said. "Well, let me check and see if you can come in and see the doctor earlier than normal." She placed me on hold. "Mrs. Burnside, what about coming in next Wednesday?" she asked.

"I'm teaching, but I can come in," I replied. I wondered if something was seriously wrong with me.

It was a beautiful day when Simmie and I went to the doctor's office. I felt peppy. The waiting room wasn't crowded as I checked in with the receptionist. She told me to come on back to see the doctor. I glanced back at Simmie. Within minutes the nurse and my doctor came into the examination room to see me. Zip and zap, the testing was over.

"Mrs. Burnside, I suspect you need a blood transfusion," my doctor said. "The testing done here shows your blood levels are too low. I want you to go to the lab for more bloodwork. Please get dressed; I'll have your paperwork sent over to the lab. Uh, if I'm diagnosing this correctly, it's a miracle that you are still alive . . . you will need a complete blood transfusion, I am sure. No matter what, I'll call you when the results of your bloodwork come in . . . tomorrow or in the next few days," he said.

"Will I make it? Is it serious?" I asked him.

"Well, yes . . . but, we can do something about it," he said, looking over my charts.

Simmie and I went to the lab on our way home so I could have the lab work done. Then we called my parents.

Mom was shocked, but Dad said, "We'll just pray. God knows. He will take care of it. We have to put everything in His hands."

When the doctor called, he said the tests confirmed his diagnosis. I needed the blood transfusion immediately because I had barely enough blood to function. He instructed me to come in for one last test so he could make sure that the right blood would be stored for my transfusion.

The day I was scheduled to come in for the last observation was changed because of technical problems with the main machine. Then I got another phone call from the doctor's office stating that they were frantic because they couldn't locate my files. Finally the files were found, and I was asked to come to the hospital early the next morning.

While Simmie waited, I was led to an examination room.

"Hello, Mrs. Burnside! It has been hard getting you back in here," said the technician as he walked into the room. "I see here that all kinds of things have happened. Your files missing, machine broke down, and a few other mishaps." He chuckled.

"Yes, that's right," I responded.

"Well, just sit there . . . I'll be back," he said, walking out the door.

I sat on the examination table and looked around the bright room. The door opened slowly, and a peaceful-looking woman peeked in and smiled at me. She had golden hair that glistened in the bright lights.

She stepped in, looked at me, and said, "Wanda, Wanda." Her voice was low, gentle, and calming. It was as if she were singing my name. She wore a soft pink uniform and had a fluffy white sweater around her shoulders. Six small gold angels adorned the shoulders of her sweater. *Wow, she must really like angels*, I thought.

She moved closer to me and smiled. Her eyes twinkled behind her golden-framed glasses. "I am here to take away this bag of blood. I must get it out of here . . . this minute!" Her voiced changed. It was as if she had a command to do this.

"Okay," I said.

She slipped over to a box and removed the bag of blood.

She held it close to her eyes and read the label. Then she stepped over to me. "This is wrong. You cannot have it!" She stared at me. My skin tingled. She held on tightly to the bag and backed her way over to the door while she continued to look at me.

Her eyes sparkled like stars in the dark night sky, but her mouth was firm and tight. She looked up at the ceiling, nodded her head, and then smiled brightly.

"Wanda . . . Wanda . . ." she said in a soft whisper. "I must leave! And this blood must go now. You are all right."

She carried the large bag of deep brownish-red blood out of my room with both of her hands.

I watched her go into the hallway of the hospital. She talked to another nurse, and they both walked quickly down the hallway. Just as they disappeared from my view, the technician walked in.

"Sorry I took so long. I was checking on a few things," he said. He walked to the box on the table and looked inside of it. "Where is your bag of blood? Where is it, Mrs. Burnside?" he demanded. Then his voice rose and he shouted, "Mrs. Burnside, did you get into this box?"

"No! The other nurse came in and got it!"

"What nurse? Who? Where is she?" he shouted.

"She just passed you in the hallway!" I said, my eyes filling with tears. It was stressful enough knowing that I had to have the transfusion without a man screaming at me!

"What hallway?" he yelled.

"This one . . . right there . . . you just passed her . . . a moment ago!"

"I saw nobody!" he shouted. He ran out of the room and looked around. He came back into my room. He ran out again. By this time, nurses were running around . . . and doctors, too!

The technician told them what had happened. The intercom blasted a warning signal. I heard, "All security be on watch . . . missing blood! Missing blood! Security, report to the third floor!"

In moments, the police, security officers, doctors, nurses, and other medical personnel filled the area with chaos.

Then, my blood technician came back into my room. He looked at me and said, "Mrs. Burnside, I need you to describe who came in here when I left."

I said, "There was a short nurse with golden hair and glasses. She was dressed in a pink uniform and wore a white sweater with lots of tiny gold angel pins on her shoulders. She smiled so . . ."

"Wait! We don't wear that color uniform in this unit. Look into the hallway. We don't dress like that!" he stated.

I looked into the hallway and saw medical personnel in green or gray uniforms. But while I was looking into the hallway, I saw more nurses with that pink uniform. They were busy around the unit desk.

"There they are!" I pointed into the hallway. "Look!"

The technician said, "I don't see them . . . where?" He shook his head and got his charts, then went into the hallway to talk to the police officers. Several of them came into my room to speak to me. I explained what happened. They questioned me more.

Suddenly, a very tall police officer came and asked the others to come with him. The police left. Then the tall officer came back with the nurse in pink! She said, "Wanda, that blood was contaminated. It would kill you. It was the wrong blood. We were sent to save your life and others on this unit. We must go. God is with you!"

I raised my hands and cried out, "Oh . . . Lord! Thank you! Thank you for saving my life! Thank you for protecting me!"

I opened my eyes when I heard angry voices in the hallway. There was a huge, thunderous discussion outside of my room. "No! No! That delivery truck was not supposed to bring that shipment of blood here. It is all contaminated with HIV! Yes! Yes! That is the highest level of contaminated . . . HIV blood bags . . . in this city! The orders were to dispose of it at . . ."

Then someone slammed my room's door shut. Next, someone came in and told me to leave and that my doctor would call me the next day. They apologized for the disturbance.

Strangely enough, when I stepped out of the room, Simmie was standing there. He asked me what was going on. Then he said that the televisions in the lobby said that there was a citywide emergency because a truckload of highly contaminated blood went to one of the local hospitals.

He took my hand. Then he said, "Wanda, did . . ."

I cried, "God saved my life! His angels came and encamped around me!"

Instead of going home, we stopped by my parents' home and told them what happened. Over dinner we all praised God together.

I had my blood transfusion, an eight-hour procedure, within days. My attending nurse wore golden angel pins on her sweater, too.

Although we go through great trials, we can be assured that Psalm 91 is true. And we can trust Psalm 34:7: "The angel of the Lord encamps around those who fear him, and he delivers them."

The Majesty of Heaven

Susan M. Watkins

I was at my breaking point. A diagnosis of severe endometriosis had ground my world to a halt as relentless pain and immobility overtook my joy and eroded my peace. Two surgeries had failed to alleviate my pain. But that Sunday morning, with flinty determination, I dressed and readied myself to pay the Lord a visit at His home.

During Sunday's worship service that chilly February morning, I sang my beliefs past the ceiling's confines. While I sang, I suddenly left my body. I found myself sheltered between two angels somewhat larger than me, who were supporting me with a gentle touch beneath each elbow. They were radiant, illuminated from within, and shining with heaven's light, yet similar in form to humans. I looked down and saw that I wore the same seamless robes as they did.

As our journey began, I was carried through earth's light-blue atmosphere in what seemed to be a small, invisible vessel. We stood, somehow centrally suspended in its interior. Despite our speed, I felt no external force against my body. I just felt a soft breeze gently moving my hair and garments.

The ascent was similar to riding an escalator at rocket velocity, yet we remained unaffected within the encapsulation. As we covered trillions of miles in nanoseconds, the atmosphere changed. The blue skies of the first heaven became varying shades of indigo, deep navy, then black. I turned to see earth shrinking behind me and its familiar orb growing dimmer. Looking beneath my feet, I realized nothing was underneath them but vast space. Though I had no structural protection, I experienced no fear.

We entered a different atmosphere studded with massive planets, space matter, and stars glowing against the midnight-black backdrop. It was the second heaven. At this point I heard greater exterior noise. We *whooshed* past innumerable stars, each one bearing the name God thoughtfully appointed to it.

I continued looking at the wonderment of my location, and my silent companions reassured me by thought. No matter how much I moved and twisted to observe things far beyond Hubble Telescope's gaze, my angels' touch was never interrupted.

Again, our speed increased and the stars became elongated streaks of light. The rocketing noise as we passed them was nearly deafening. I surveyed the expanse again and knew we must be in very deep space, as it was devoid of the planets I had seen earlier.

Our course never changed, remaining straight with diagonal altitude. This was a very intentional route; I realized this was the highway between heaven and earth. The blurred starlight reduced to specks of light. We entered a completely black area of space, absent of all stars, planets, and any astronomical matter. Then we abruptly changed course and moved vertically at a slower pace.

We burst into the spectacular white light of the third heaven. It had the same coloring as my angels but saturated the atmosphere in every direction. We entered what appeared to be an enormous square room that had no ceiling or walls. It stretched miles in every direction and had a vaporous floor.

I could see an elevated platform in the far distance, in the center of the room. As we neared, I realized it was God's throne. When we reached the halfway point from the room's entrance to the throne, my escorts stopped and directed me to advance closer. The guides then left my side and returned to flank a type of doorway where we had entered.

I paused, wondering why I was to continue alone, then found I could walk unaided without ever touching the floor. I literally walked on nothing. Excitedly closing the distance between God and myself, I began to evaluate my ethereal surroundings.

Spice-filled incense, with heavy notes of myrrh, permeated the vast room, and I knew this was the same recipe Moses burned in God's earthly tabernacle centuries earlier. The fragrance emitted a sense of holiness. The cavernous room was saturated with power. It was a shimmering vision; the atmosphere was wholly electrified. God's power somehow transferred to the surrounding space, and when the atmosphere reached the saturation point, the discharge of this power appeared to burst with sparkling light in displays of grandeur. This outpouring of power filled the entirety of the throne room with an uninterrupted symphony of glittering light dotting every available space.

Advancing on my journey, I heard the sound of purest worship coming from somewhere over my right shoulder. It, too, was holy, with countless voices declaring God's sacredness. The music felt alive. This worship never ceased and bathed the environment.

The throne room was filled with angelic armies of various sizes and responsibilities, myriads blurring into the distance. They moved about freely without colliding. There was complete order and peace. As I walked closer to the throne, I observed angels serving and surrounding God. The Father's majesty saturated every space with magnificence.

Invited again to draw near to God, I stationed myself at three-quarters of the distance from the door. I knew it was the closest I could approach at that time. The light emanating from God was blinding yet caused no discomfort. It was so brilliant that I couldn't distinguish His face, only His massive form. The throne was elevated on a circular platform with ascending steps crafted from white stone. The abstract halo bathing His presence flowed to the right, and smaller angels, still larger than humans, flew in and out of the incense curtain, capturing something tangible in golden bowls and bringing it directly to God. I realized these were the prayers of God's redeemed children.

Much larger angels flew around the perimeter of the throne. The smaller angels continued collecting prayers, disturbing the flow of incense before the incense quickly reestablished its own structure.

I stood awestruck, witnessing God resting on His throne, entirely in command of His creation. As I watched, the Lord unexpectedly grew brighter and released brilliant rays of light straight from His body that arced across the room. Similar to smooth lightning bolts, the closest ones went in multiple directions, spanning fifty to one hundred feet, while larger ones went into the far distance before disappearing into the gossamer floor.

This display never ceased, and the power arcs landed everywhere except where I stood. With their release, bursts of continued light intensified until the massive room shone with glory. The expanding release seemed deafening; however, I knew the Almighty was harnessing full disclosure.

Being entrusted to record His majesty and taste the smallest bite of what is prepared for His bride was an unexpected honor and revelation. I was encouraged to thoroughly evaluate my surroundings, assess the activity, listen to the worship and note its accompanying music, smell the fragrances, and feel and see the power He alone houses.

I watched the angels passionately collect infinite prayers, constantly moving in and out of the swirling incense and delivering one prayer after another to Father God's careful attention. After reviewing each petition, He alone decided its answer and timing—sending that angel immediately out of the room to travel thousands of light years in seconds to earth, bearing God's awaited answer. Prayers were answered immediately, and those answers were delivered to earth, but while some were instantaneous interventions, others needed synchronization with our time and seasonal governances before their release. There was no delay in the answer, just the perfection of its release for each individual need.

Since I had absorbed all I was capable of comprehending in my finite form, God now engaged me. It was time to address my visit.

His personal love enveloped me like the incense surrounding Him. Its unfathomable depth somehow became a living, infused part of me. I've never known such love from any human, and in that wondrously peaceful moment, deep called unto deep. We communicated without ever uttering a word, discussing my entire experience. He revealed that I had incomplete assignments and promised healing for my progressively debilitating disease. My barrenness would likewise be lifted, and a son, needed for His plans, would be born.

Realizing my window was closing, I begged to remain. Again, He told me that my assignments were unfinished. None but I could execute what I was born to do. Pierced, I knew I must return. Thoughts of leaving my precious heavenly Father distressed me, yet the imperfect beckoned.

Taking a prolonged last look, I had a miniscule understanding of Christ's choice. Leaving the glory of heaven for thirty-three years of earth's dust was a decision fueled entirely by His sacrificial love for us. Like Moses cocooned in his rocky cleft, I, too, was granted a glimpse of God passing by. My angelic escorts reappeared and touched each elbow, and we were instantly gone.

I was immediately back in my upright body at church, though singing along to a different song. No one suspected I'd been gone, much less that I'd just been standing before God's holy throne. Life as I'd understood it was delightfully changed.

Exactly as promised, two weeks later I was miraculously healed, and my scarred womb was opened. The following year my promised son cooed in my arms, a reminder of the Lord's faithfulness.

Eternal purpose continues to direct my calling, yet I ever yearn for the splendor of my Father's home.

A Visit to Heaven

Melissa Henderson

On a cool, crisp Wednesday morning in 2007, my husband and I received an upsetting phone call from the nursing home where my eighty-six-year-old mama lived. The nurse reported that when she went to help Mama prepare for the day, she found her unresponsive. Since a DNR (do not resuscitate) order was in place, the nurse asked about contacting the local rescue squad to take Mama to the hospital. We gave permission to call for help and have her transported. It was a heart-wrenching time. We were filled with panic and worry as we prepared to go see Mama in her town two hours away from where we lived.

While on the road, we received another phone call and learned from the nursing home staff that she had not been transferred to the hospital yet.

The rescue squad personnel had arrived and assessed her condition. They had suggested that she stay in her own bed, as she may not be comfortable in unfamiliar surroundings at the hospital. They gave her oxygen and monitored her. She was resting peacefully, and we were told this would be the best treatment for her.

When we arrived at her room, we wanted to rush in, yet at the same time we hesitated, afraid of what we would see. I placed my palm on the cold silver door handle and entered.

I instantly noted that Mama's complexion was pale and gray. She was still unresponsive. The nursing staff explained that they believed she'd had a major stroke. Though there had been no change in her status, she actually looked comfortable, with her pink nightgown tucked into fresh, clean white sheets.

Lights were dimmed, and the mood was peaceful yet somber. Somehow the lowered lights seemed to ease everyone's pain. My sisters and their husbands arrived, and the family spoke in quiet voices to Mama, whispering words of love and thankfulness. Each of us, one at a time, gently rubbed her hands and stroked her hair. These simple acts comforted us.

Soon the doctor arrived and explained to us that the end was near. It was time to say good-bye and make arrangements.

Mama's beautiful face was now distorted and her breathing shallow; she was still unresponsive.

We learned that people were praying throughout the nursing home. We spoke with friends and other family members, and we learned prayer chains had been contacted. Our family was thankful for the concern and love pouring in.

Time stood still as we waited, watched, and prayed. The clock on the wall ticked, each moment feeling heavier than the last. Eventually several nurses entered, asking us to step outside the room so they could reposition Mama.

Our steps were cautious and our hearts shaky as we moved to the hallway in silence. Staring at the hard, brown tile floor, some of us were quiet, while some spoke a few words. Tears flowed while we waited to return to Mama. Finally, the door opened and a nurse walked out, looking alarmed.

"Please go in . . . and see for yourself."

We were confused and concerned. What was happening?

Apprehensively, we entered the room to see Mama sitting up in her hospital bed as alert as she'd ever been in her life. "Well, hello. What are you all doing here?"

Imagine our surprise! We'd been told to prepare for the worst, and here was Mama, sitting up and talking like nothing unusual had occurred. Her beautiful face was no longer distorted. Her skin was a glowing pink.

The doctor shook her head and tried to find some explanation, saying when things like this happen, there is really no known reason. In our hearts, we knew differently. People had prayed, and those prayers had been answered.

As we filled Mama in on what had happened—the unresponsiveness, the times her breathing stopped—she became nervous and distraught. She told us she knew she had died. She spoke of seeing Daddy, who had gone to heaven on Easter Sunday 1998.

She described how he looked in his dark suit, white dress shirt, and tie—handsome as always. He had held out an open hand and asked her to go with him. But as much as she wanted to be with Daddy and in heaven, this was not her time.

Mama kept mentioning the "babies" who helped her come back to us. We finally realized the babies were angels. She spoke of seeing those babies and their sweetness and kindness.

During the day, Mama cried at various times, wondering if Daddy was upset with her for not going with him. We reassured Mama that God would come for her when the time was right.

Doctors shared with us that this truly was a miracle. Mama had lived through this ordeal and only suffered very small side effects from this major stroke.

Our family knows God answers prayers. Sometimes the answer is yes, sometimes it's no, and sometimes it's not now. And we were glad that day that the answer was yes to Mama remaining alive.

That day we also learned lessons of patience, kindness, trust, and faith. People who weren't sure of the power of prayer told us about their own faith journey and how this miracle inspired and comforted them.

Mama stayed with us six more years, going to heaven one week before her ninety-second birthday. We miss her and Daddy very much but know we will see them one day in heaven. For now, we know Mama is with Daddy in the loving presence of God.

The Gray Caterpillar

Alyssa Roat

"Just breathe in deeply."

The machines beeped and the prongs *whooshed* in my nose. In seconds, I would be out cold.

I wasn't concerned. Braces were an annoying part of being thirteen, and teeth that wanted to grow backward in my head were, too. In fact, the nastiness of it gave my middle-school mind a perverse sense of joy.

"Yeah," I told my friends, "my canines are still up in my head, and they want to grow backward and come through the roof of my mouth like a shark's teeth, so they have to drill up in there and glue chains on them and pull them down the right way."

My church friends squealed satisfyingly, and my softball teammates showed a pleasing amount of fascination. The best part was that I would have those stupid braces off in a year; at least only part of my freshman experience would be marred by metal teeth.

Not that braces were my biggest worry. They were just easier to focus on. When I thought about them, they gave me a sense of the future, as if I really was going to live.

What if something goes wrong, and I die while I'm under? I thought apathetically. *That would be convenient.*

Sure, my life seemed great. My softball career was advancing apace; my club team was doing well. I was almost two hundred pages into writing my first novel. I helped out at church. I was taking high school credits to get ahead.

But what did any of that matter?

Dark whispers came to me at night. *Your life is worthless. You're just a drain on the earth's resources. You're incapable of helping advance the kingdom. Look at you! How many people have you led to Jesus? Ah, yes. None.* I woke up in the morning more tired than when I went to bed.

Those dark voices followed me throughout the day. *Shut up!* I screamed at them. *Go away!*

You can't make us, they snickered. *We'll never leave. We'll never stop until you give up your worthless life and die.*

There were so many nightmares—of skeletal beasts trying to devour me under a blood-red sky or claws clinging to my ankle, trying to pull me into an abyss as I clutched the ledge.

Why do I bother? I asked myself. *My life is a detriment to society. I'm incapable of doing anything for the kingdom. Maybe I should die.*

Of course, I didn't think I would be happy in death. The voices repeated until I believed them: *You can't be accepted into heaven. You hear us. You listen to us. That means you're tainted. You will never be allowed in heaven.*

Lord, I prayed, *before I die, or even because of my death, please bring my friends to you.*

I wondered, sometimes, if I staged my death to look like an accident, if I left behind a notebook full of my love for God and my excitement to know Him in life or death, whether it would trigger in my friends an existential crisis that would lead them to God. Maybe by dying I could do something good before I spent the rest of my existence in hell. I was willing to do it, if it would work.

So oral surgery was no big deal. Physical pain in general wasn't. It could only hurt my body, and most of the time, I felt like I'd halfway left it behind already.

The anesthesia kicked in, I suppose, because they started rooting around in my mouth. Then I was seeing the procedure from a place outside my head, right above it. Their faces were blurred, their words distorted. Then I was somewhere else.

There were boxes everywhere. It was like a shipping warehouse, everything conveying a sense of movement, though in reality, I couldn't see the boxes moving at all. There were no light sources, only a soft brown warmth. But then I looked up.

Far up there was a light, the most blindingly cool, pure-white light like I'd never seen before and didn't know could exist. As I looked at it, I felt crushed as if boulders were pressing on every inch of me and my insides were made of lead. No one told me, but I knew. It was the agony of a depraved existence, an agony I didn't fully realize I was in. And if I could only reach that light, my pain would be gone. I just had to let go.

Hello.

It wasn't really a word, more a transmission of the idea of a greeting. I was strangely calm when confronted by the thought projection of a light-gray caterpillar taller than me, looking at me with a human face.

I want to go up there, I told it. But again, there was no sound. It was a transmission of knowledge that transcended words.

It's not time yet.

No. I can't take this anymore.

It's not time yet, the caterpillar repeated. It handed me a light. It said nothing, but I knew I had to follow the light, follow it back to my body.

The light led me down. Down through inky passages formed completely of darkness with paths leading sightlessly into the blackness. Every cell of my body was in agony. I wanted to go back, but I couldn't. If I turned around, I would be lost in the darkness forever, the darkness where familiar voices whispered.

I descended into the room. They were calling my name, telling me it was time to wake up. I settled back in.

I was jolted back to physical reality by my body shaking and convulsing, my teeth clacking together even through the gauze stuffed in my mouth. My vision swirled with colors, and the walls seemed to be melting into liquid. I vaguely sensed anxiety in the room. I heard people speaking. They thought I didn't hear. "Is this normal?" the intern asked.

"No. This has never happened before," someone else replied.

Then my brain settled into the function one would expect of someone who had been under anesthesia.

My next clear memories are of attempting to walk out of the room after refusing a wheelchair. I fell over and had to be wheeled out anyway. I climbed into the car tipsily and made garbled, affirmative noises through the gauze to my mom, assuring her I was okay, and we drove home, where life continued as usual other than me icing my mouth and subsisting on liquids and soft foods.

But in another sense, life didn't continue as usual. I didn't know where I had been in the room with the boxes and the caterpillar, but I knew people weren't supposed to dream under anesthesia. I knew my mom mentioned it took them an extra hour to wake me up after they said I would be ready. No one told me, but I knew what that light was. I knew I had almost died.

Now, I know there's just as much chance that I reacted weirdly to the anesthesia and had a strange dream. But at the time, I couldn't believe it was anything other than supernatural. Almost dying wasn't a big deal. The out-of-body experience didn't faze me much, either. But one phrase kept echoing through my head: *It's not time yet.*

I was inches from heaven. I saw the light, as cliché as that seemed. I witnessed a taste of glory by realizing that the awful pain in which humans currently existed, whether they were aware of it or not, would be lifted away by heaven's light. And I even knew, in that moment, that the light was home, where I belonged. There was no way I was going to hell. But again, there was that statement: *It's not time yet.*

It wasn't time to die. Not yet. And if I was that close to heaven and was still sent back to earth, that meant there was a reason. My continued existence on earth meant one very important thing: God still had things for me to do. We weren't finished yet.

Not dying takes away a lot of fear. I'd been there already, so what on earth could I be afraid of? Besides, I had a purpose. I had things to do until that day when my Father drew me into the light and said, "Well done, my good and faithful servant."

That doesn't mean the voices never whispered again. But they could never again convince me that my Father didn't want me.

I didn't share my experience with anyone in its entirety, and snippets only with a few. It was bizarre, and getting hung up on it didn't matter. What mattered was my limited time to tell as many people about Jesus as possible.

I never felt like I was doing amazing things. I lived my life and did my best to serve God. The voices kept whispering how terrible I was, how I should stop, how I made no difference. But that just made me cling to Him even harder and charge forward.

Then one day I graduated from high school. My childhood was over; soon I would be living on my own on the other side of the country with no one I knew in the entire state, let alone in the town. And I looked back on that chapter of my life, the chapter between wanting to die and graduating.

I saw over one hundred led to Christ.

I saw over one thousand spoken to about the Word. I saw little eyes brightening with understanding.

I saw prayers over those who were crying, encouragement for those who wanted to give up.

I saw the gap-toothed grins of the homeless, clutching new Bibles to their chests. I heard thunderous laughter as the friendless man at the bus station told me his jokes and cracked himself up. I saw the woman who sobbed with happiness because I gave her a granola bar, just because no one else had cared. I felt her arms around me and her tears on my shoulder, saw her beaming smile when I sat and listened to her and prayed for her, when even her own daughter had deserted her. To this day, I still don't know her name.

I heard girls asking me why I was so happy. I heard them asking questions about my faith. I heard surprised exclamations of, "You're not a hypocrite!" Even if I didn't see them dedicate their lives to Jesus, that doesn't mean they never did.

So many small encounters. The man I gave a pack of gum to as I apologized because it was the only thing I had. And he smiled at me, thanked me heartfully, and I knew it wasn't the gum that mattered. It was my eyes meeting his, acknowledging him.

Maybe I had a miraculous encounter. Maybe I didn't. In the end, it doesn't matter. I was no Billy Graham or child saint. I made some bad decisions and some selfish ones. But I lived. I accepted the gift of life God gave me. And that was what mattered.

The Judgment Seat in Heaven

Rose Alexander

I stood at the top of the stairs to a dark basement below. The door was firmly closed; there was no turning back. Intuitively I knew the steps led down to my former earthly existence, which was now barred forever. That life was done, and I was content with that. Although I had left deeply loved by family and friends, I would not see them again—on earth, at least. One day we might meet in heaven. But at the moment, I was mainly concerned with my new self and location.

I fearlessly turned to assess the transition. I knew my physical self had died, freeing my spirit to enter the afterlife. A Christian for many years, I had no deep fear of what I might encounter, only mild anxiety and uncertainty. What would happen next?

It was no coincidence that my earthly life had been depicted as a shadowy existence in murky depths. I was raised in a dysfunctional family, and my mother had taken my sister, my two brothers, and me to church off and on. When I was ten, I had come to the awareness of God as our heavenly Father and Jesus as His Son. A few months after I turned eleven, my sister—eleven months younger—and I went forward in church, responding to the pastor's altar call as the Lord beckoned our spirits. She and I professed our commitment of faith and prayed with Pastor Dave Burnham at The Chapel on Fir Hill in Akron, Ohio. A few days later, we began receiving Bible lessons in the mail that would draw us into God's Word for answers and knowledge. At sunrise service on Easter Sunday morning, we were baptized and began our public lives as Christians.

As dedicated as we first were, we could not completely overcome negative family influences and behaviors. Although my sister and I went to church and Sunday school, we did not attend regularly.

As a teenager, I got caught up with the wrong people and in a secular worldview. Then I repented after a few years and again found my place on the lifelong journey leading to God. I had certainly stumbled and would reap serious consequences for years to come.

When I was twenty-one, I married. Seven years and two sons later, I divorced my husband when I discovered his flagrant adultery. For the next five years, I focused on raising my sons and earning a couple of college degrees. At age thirty-three, I married a Christian man I met at a Bible study. By the time I was thirty-nine, we had added two more children to our family and had fully embarked on professional career paths. As church members, we hosted a home Bible study, and I assisted with the women's ministry while also teaching Sunday school part-time. Our lives seemed full and complete, and I felt secure in my faith for the first time in my life.

However, Satan has a way of pulling the rug out from under you just when things seem to be going well. My marriage began to crumble as my husband decided it took too much effort for us to get along. Although we had many valuable similarities, our differences impacted important parts of our marriage and family. Despite on-and-off-again marital counseling, I filed for separation, and he filed for divorce. By age fifty-two, I was on the threshold of starting over again. Although emotionally fragile and spiritually depleted, I knew the Lord had not abandoned me. I had tried to walk faithfully with Him each step of the way since rededicating my life to Him at age thirty, a few years before my second marriage. But maybe my foot had slipped on the climb of faith. I could not be sure whether I was in the right or wrong of our failed marriage, but I realized I had to strengthen my spiritual ties to our church, which my ex-husband had left, and continue to care for our children, the youngest of whom was fifteen. It was a difficult time when I began to doubt everything in my life: my faith, my strength, and my wisdom. Failure after failure were the milestones of my path as I looked back upon decades of poor decisions and selfish behavior.

The next few years passed quickly, and like a ship in the doldrums that senses a breeze in its sails, my faith began to soar, restoring my hope for a fruitful future. God was surely with me, and I was returning fully to Him through Bible study, prayer, and ministry.

I had generally enjoyed good health, so when symptoms of an internal problem manifested, I immediately scheduled a medical appointment. The doctor confirmed I would need a colonoscopy to diagnose the problem. A previous test six years before had been clear, but another was now scheduled.

Although a bit nervous, I reminded myself that God was in control and He would determine the outcome. The test went smoothly. In the recovery room, the doctor told me he had found a polyp. "This is the kind that turns to cancer if we leave it," he said, "so I removed it."

I was grateful. My grandfather and an aunt had faced colon cancer. It was good to have my problem addressed.

My adult son drove me home after the exam, and I told him I would be fine the rest of the day.

"I'll just rest in my bedroom," I told him. "The anesthetic has mostly worn off; I'm just a little woozy."

He wanted to stay with me, but I sent him home with reassurances that I would be fine. Lying in bed with my head on the pillow, I fell into a deep sleep quickly and effortlessly—as though I had fallen into a trance.

That was where the dream or vision began.

In my vision I emerged from the dark, dirty basement of the lower-middle-class home where I had grown up. For a time, our parents had kept a dog down there, so the concrete floor was littered with dog feces and urine that my mother cleaned up now and then. There might have also been rats living in an adjoining room.

I was relieved to leave that dark, odorous basement with the door firmly closed behind me. Subconsciously, I knew the basement represented more than my childhood; it was the symbol of my earthly life—full of darkness and fearsome things I could not control as a child but had tried to escape as an adult.

Now, turning to view my spiritual destiny, I met waves of mist too thick to see through, yet not deeply opaque like fog. The mist extended all around me; I had no idea how big the place was or how far it reached. I just knew that I was in heaven, and it was not at all what I had expected.

I had assumed heaven would be a bustling place. Upon passing from this life, I would arrive at the golden gates, which were guarded by an archangel or two, or perhaps Saint

Peter. I would give the password somehow acknowledging Jesus as Savior, the gates would open, and I would enter, rushing to embrace God and then to find my loved ones.

But this was very different. The mist was so bright that it was like a nuclear explosion—pure, unadulterated light all around—dazzling and blindingly bright. The light was enough to humble me, but that was not all.

I heard a low buzzing sound—voices! They were approaching from within a deeper area of the mist. It was a crowd, but were they coming to welcome or reject me? Suddenly I was afraid—not completely, because I was secure in my salvation. But the reality of meeting God and the heavenly citizens was overwhelming. What would I say?

The swirling mist began to part, and I slowly made out the forms and shapes of individuals. They were not clearly distinct, still absorbed in the mist. In their midst, I knew, was God. There was no escaping this meeting. No one stood with me. I faced Him alone.

I bowed my head as the throng drew closer and paused before me. I could not meet His eyes because I was so unworthy. Ashamed of my misdeeds, I did not deserve His consideration. I was a nothing, and I deserved nothing. Trembling, I did not look up at Him.

Suddenly, a man stood beside me in a flowing robe. He, too, was facing the crowd that stood opposite. I felt strength and power in the man's stance. But there was gentleness and love, too.

I nearly wept with joy. Jesus was my Advocate! No longer alone, I had the best and only possible Redeemer at my side. My fear retreated, and peace began to overtake me. Finally, I was truly safe and secure, now for all eternity.

The next moment I woke up. I felt sad that the dream or vision, whatever it was, had ended. Had I really died and gone to heaven to face judgment? Had Jesus stood beside me as atonement for all my sins?

It didn't matter because I had seen with clarity what my soul has always known since the day I became aware of saving grace. One day I will face divine judgment, as will everyone. On that day I will rest securely, knowing that I made the right decision when I accepted Jesus' death on the cross as payment for my sins. I am saved for all eternity from the just and awesome and fearful judgment of God.

Angel in the Parking Lot

LAURIE ALLRED BOYD

It was the summer of 1977, and there we were in Newark, New Jersey—two seventeen-year-old country girls who had just flown across the United States from Oregon to join the America's Youth in Concert group, except no one was at the airport to meet us. We called the academy sponsoring us several times, but no one answered. It was getting later and later, and no one came, so we assumed the employees at the academy must have gone home for the day. Since we had a month of travel across Europe ahead and limited finances, we decided to get a room for the night at the cheapest motel we could find on the airport's announcement board. We called the motel, and the desk clerk said he would send a shuttle to pick us up.

At around eight o'clock, a thirty-something man with long hair and a scruffy beard showed up driving an older car. As we traveled to the motel, being rather innocent young ladies, we eagerly talked about the tour and no one from the academy meeting us at the airport. As we drove along, the buildings became a little more run-down, we saw more garbage on the roads, and the people hanging around in front of stores with bars on the windows seemed a little rougher than I was used to. Little alarm bells began to go off in my head.

We finally arrived at the U-shaped complex, and no other cars were in the parking lot. We were not as eager to share our life stories at this point. The desk clerk was another thirty-something man. He gave us a room three doors down from the main office. We had not eaten since lunch on the plane, about nine hours earlier, so we asked if the kitchen was open. It was not, so we walked to our room with rumbling stomachs.

The weather was very hot and muggy, and the motel room had a swamp cooler instead of a proper air conditioner. We turned it on and continued to sweat, although we had a breeze to sweat in now. The motel room was as hot as it was outside, but we were not going to open the window. The phone rang, and the desk clerk asked if we would like to go get some dinner with him and the driver. I kindly declined, then put the desk chair under the doorknob.

My friend and I decided to try to sleep, so we put on our pajamas and prayed for protection. As I drifted off to sleep in that muggy, hot room, in my mind's eye, it was as if I were standing in the parking lot looking at the area outside of our motel room, and there, leaning back against the wall to the right of our room's door was an angel. He was so tall his head almost touched the overhang, and his soft, blond hair brushed the tops of his shoulders. His robe was white, overlaid with another robe the color of glacial-lake water. His arms were crossed over his chest, and his ankles were crossed as he leaned against the wall, slowly scanning the area, left and right, left and right, guarding us. I slept peacefully all night. In the morning when I woke up, before I could say anything, my friend said, "Laurie, you will never guess what I saw just before I fell asleep last night . . ." She perfectly described the angel I'd seen.

I knew a psalm talked about God being with you wherever you are, so I looked it up. It was Psalm 139. When we exited our room, the men from the previous night were gone, and an elderly man and his wife checked us out of our room. Then the man drove us back to the airport, where we finally connected with the people from the academy.

After practicing with the choir for a couple of days, we performed on July 4 at the Independence Hall pavilion; then we sang in Carnegie Hall. After the Carnegie performance, we caught a red-eye flight to London, England, the first of many stops across Europe. I looked out the airplane window over that vast expanse of water as the sun rose and the light reflected in the clouds floated under the plane in pink, purple, and golden hues. As I gazed down at the watery world, the words of Psalm 139 echoed in my thoughts: "Where can I go from your Spirit? Where can I flee from your presence? If I go up to the heavens, you are there; if I make my bed in the depths, you are there. If I rise on the wings of the dawn, if I settle on the far side of the sea, even there your hand will guide me, your right hand will hold me fast" (vv. 7–10).

Until that moment, I had not truly grasped that God is everywhere, that the Spirit travels with us, and that I can never outrun God, because He is already where I am and where I am going. I realized that this passage refers not only to the physical space my body occupies, but also to where I am in my relationship with Him. He promised that He would be with me, guide me, and never let me go.

As we sang our way across Europe with the concert tour over the next month, I knew with a lifetime of confidence that God traveled with us and that He had assigned one of His angels to protect us all along the way on the far side of the sea.

Praying with the Angels

SHARILYNN HUNT

The early morning alarm startled my brain awake. Before turning over to catch a few more minutes of sleep, I realized, *It's Monday!*

That's the day my friend and prayer partner, Shirley, and I prayed together. We were a team. She directed the church kindergarten program while I headed up the preschool program.

Both of our homes were within a few minutes' drive of our small Alabama church. Each week we knelt in the sanctuary to petition our Lord for the needs of the children's ministries. The picturesque country church was on a historical registry and nestled among modern homes and new subdivisions. For generations, local families had gathered for services.

Not living near any of our relatives, my husband and I loved this small congregation filled with people who embraced us. They even treated our young children like their own grandchildren. My Monday times with Shirley added another layer of spiritual development through the power of intercessory prayer. We always left with our faith energized, which made the early morning effort worthwhile.

While my family slept in their cozy beds, I threw on my clothes and left the warm house, going into the winter chill. As I drove down the dark street, I noted the stillness of the morning. A dim light began to creep over the horizon.

I turned into the empty parking lot. Where was Shirley? We usually arrived around the same time. The deserted street showed no signs of her headlights. I remained in the heated car, noticing that deep shadows from overhead tree limbs covered the pavement. The small cemetery next to the church parking lot stood in semidarkness under the towering trees.

After waiting a few more minutes, I decided to go in and turn on the church lights to prepare for our prayer time. The bitter cold bit my face as I headed up the back stairs of the church to the dark entrance. I reminded myself, *I'm here and committed to pray—even if it's just me.*

I fumbled with the lock and pushed open the creaking back door. The sound echoed throughout the silent building. My footsteps thumped on the old wooden floors of the small fellowship room. When I flipped the light switch, my eyes darted right and left for any sign of movement while I held my coat tightly. I tried not to shiver from the cold and uneasiness of being alone. Should I have waited in the car after all?

When I entered the sanctuary, soft rays of light streamed through the frosted windows onto the dark-red carpet. Even when I turned on the overhead lights, uneasy emotions stirred within me, but I kept reminding myself, *God is here!*

All the empty pews were a direct contrast to the one hundred filled spaces during Sunday services. My anxious thoughts seemed out of place in such a tranquil and peaceful environment.

Kneeling in front of the first pew, I focused on my prayer mission. My commitment to pray for the concerns of the week absorbed me. When I began to worship, my body relaxed. Minutes passed while praises left my lips.

Though God participated in my prayer conversation with Him, He was not visible. Then, however, I had a feeling of being watched. My eyes opened, and I was allowed to see into the supernatural realm. I gasped. Angels! In every pew throughout the sanctuary. And so many of them squeezed into the room! Did I need protection, or were they sent to give me prayer support?

The angels wore shimmering white robes with a translucent glow around them as if veils covered their faces and bodies. Their brightness allowed me to see them and look through them at the same time. They were huge! As if called to attention, these heavenly beings sat shoulder to shoulder in an upright position. They had to be at least five or six feet tall while sitting down! Their angelic wings were not visible to me, or maybe they were just tucked behind them.

Did God always send angels to support one young woman's conversation with her Lord? Vibrant energy of love and acceptance flowed from them. I sensed they knew my heart's desires and were in one accord with my praises and petitions. Yet their overpowering presence made me more aware of the contrast between their supernatural, heavenly substance and my smaller body made up of blood and bones. Goose bumps covered my arms, and I became frightened. When the angel Gabriel visited Mary of Nazareth, she was afraid, yet the angel talked to her.

Even though the angels remained silent, God's love and presence filled the place. I closed my eyes. When I reopened them, my eyes could no longer see the angelic beings. But the atmosphere felt charged with their existence. My hands trembled from this supernatural experience. No longer able to pray, I got up and hurried from the room.

Within minutes, I locked the building and rushed to my car. Driving home, I thought, *How foolish to be afraid*. Why had these angels come? Had God said, "Hey, I need you to pray with Shari since she will be all alone this morning?" Smiling, I realized that whatever the reason, a band of angels came for prayer on a cold winter morning as my backup.

When I got home, my husband stood in the kitchen, preparing breakfast. I said, "Honey, I've got to tell you about morning prayer! Then I need to call Shirley."

"Are they not all ministering spirits, sent forth to minister for them who shall be heirs of salvation?" (Hebrews 1:14 KJV).

Catching a Wave with Heavenly Help

Martin Ziegner

It was August of 1968. I was out of school for the month and went to California to visit a friend in Los Angeles. One day he told me that we should go to the beach because there had been a storm on the Pacific Ocean. He said, "The waves should be really big!" I don't remember which beach we went to, but it was a beautiful California summer day. And on the sand was a stunning panorama of SoCal girls in bikinis, so it didn't really register with me that only a few brave souls were in the water and the lifeguard stations had red flags flying over them.

Looking out over the ocean, I saw three- to five-foot (and occasionally larger) waves rolling in and mostly breaking on the shore. There was what looked like a fogbank offshore, which became denser off to my right. I asked my friend about it, and he said it arose from the much larger waves breaking far offshore and we wouldn't have to worry about them because they were so distant. While looking out at them I felt an odd, periodic "thump" in my chest and a simultaneous tickling feeling on my feet. I'd never experienced anything like it and just stood there for a while feeling the thump and tickle.

Then it dawned on me that the thump was the sensation of the impacting energy of the waves breaking far in the distance and traveling to the beach. It was resonating in my chest cavity and bouncing the sand into the air, which then fell on the tops of my bare feet. I figured those must be some monster waves to have such an effect from that distance. I was happy that we wouldn't be anywhere near them.

When I went into the water I was surprised by how cold and deep it was—twelve to fifteen feet from shore it was well over six feet deep. I stayed in the water for about twenty minutes, body surfing the waves near the shore, or so I thought. Being in these waves was confusing, as they seemed to come from the left, from the right, and from directly in front of me. I was now getting cold and turned back toward the shore to orient myself. To my horror I saw that I was hundreds of yards from the shore, which was receding rapidly from view.

I realized that I was in a rip current heading for the open ocean—a terrifying realization! Just then I heard what sounded like a deep growl in the water behind me. I turned and saw that the sound came from the turbulence in the water as it rushed out to sea to feed the face of a huge wave rushing in. I had been dragged by the rip current out to that distant place I had seen from shore where the storm-generated waves were breaking on a sandbar.

An enormous wave broke directly on top of me, drove me into the sandbar, and then held me under water for what seemed like forever. I came to the surface just in time to see another wave ready to crash down onto me again. By the fourth time this happened, full-scale panic had set in, and I tried to swim toward the shore. But I was so cold and exhausted and could barely move. Sinking below the surface for that fourth time, I was certain I was about to die.

As I sank, I thought about the last breath that I held. Should I hold it as long as possible, or should I just blow it out and get on with the business of drowning? It didn't matter; either way, I was about to drown. While I struggled with the question, a phrase popped into my mind: "Father, into your hands I commit . . ." But interrupting my thought, a voice spoke directly into my right ear, "No—not now." Was it the voice of Jesus or an angel? I wasn't sure, but it was loud and distinct. I felt like He was standing behind me and holding my waist.

I then felt a tremendous upward acceleration, like being shot out of a cannon, and popped to the surface. Praise God—I could draw another breath! Strangely, I found myself standing on top of the wave, not on the face of the wave, but just behind the crest. Yet somehow I was being carried along by the wave itself. I was not swimming—just being carried along by something supporting me on the water's surface. I looked along the crest to my left and saw the wave begin to break in the distance. As the break proceeded toward me, I feared that I would again be thrown underwater, but the break stopped just as it reached my position.

As that last section broke, the deafening impact sent an explosion of spray and foam into the sky, where it hung for a moment, caught the sunlight, and refracted into a cloud of pink and gold. It was incredibly—unconceivably—beautiful! But all I could think was, *Wow, that's really pretty*. At that moment, that same voice I had heard clearly before said, "Yes, isn't this a beautiful day?" I didn't know how to respond;

drowning was not my idea of a beautiful day. I was too exhausted to swim. I didn't see how I could get off the wave and onto shore. I finally just gave up and said, "Lord, if you say it's a beautiful day—then it *is* a beautiful day!"

The wave and I were now approaching the shore, and I saw that it would break directly on the beach. Getting slammed into wet sand was not my idea of fun! The wave started to break and threw me over the crest and halfway to the sand when . . . everything simply stopped. I was looking up into the concave face of the wave and down at the glistening wet sand. The only thing moving was the base of the wave, where the water danced forward, the base of the wave catching up with the crest. It engulfed me and, with what sounded like a sigh, washed me gently onto the beach! I tried to pull myself up higher onto the beach but had absolutely no strength and passed out.

I don't know how long I lay there. When I regained consciousness I was sticky with dried salt, and kelp was stuck to my chest. My friend came running up and said how excited he was and how great the body surfing had been. But I was too stunned to speak. He said we should get something to eat, and suddenly I was ravenous.

I was able to stand up and looked up and down the beach for my shirt, shoes, and wallet. I didn't see them and wondered how I would ever find them again on the vastness of the beach because I had moved so far from my starting point. And then I looked at the ground fewer than six feet in front of me, and there were my belongings! The wave had carried me back to the exact point at which I had entered the water.

It was quite a long time before I could even talk about this experience. That was mostly because I thought no one would believe me and partially because I felt guilty that I had survived. What had I ever done to deserve such a rescue?

Eventually I realized that God's acts of grace are not something we deserve or earn—that they are not about us at all. They are all about Him, and He does those things that please Him for His own reasons, in His own time, and in His own way, and He owes no one an explanation.

Someday I hope to understand fully, but meanwhile, Jesus' words ring true: "I am with you always, even to the end of the world" (Matthew 28:20 TLB). At this point in my life, if you were to ask me where I would most like to be, my answer would be simple: in my Savior's arms—riding a wave—heading home.

And yes, that will be a beautiful day!

A Heavenly Messenger

C. F. Sherrow

I wracked my brain for a logical explanation, but nothing in my years of scientific training offered an answer. No theory, no hypothesis, not even an educated guess.

Something was standing in front of me. It didn't feel evil. And it didn't feel like a person, either.

Our Saturday evening Bible study had started off routinely: announcements, greeting one another, music. Externally, all was at peace. Internally, however, I was in turmoil. My good friend was dying. And he was convinced that God was mad at him, even hated him for all he had done. Or not done.

Jim and I had known each other for nine years. We met when he was assigned to be my clinical mentor for my first position as a physician assistant in internal medicine. I loved working with Jim during those weeks as he shared his experience and knowledge with me. A true encourager, he never made the "newbie" feel inadequate.

He'd led a pretty tough life. His demanding father had died when Jim was still quite young. Jim had been estranged from his alcoholic mother for many years. He'd been married and divorced twice. His second wife had betrayed and left him, even though he'd adopted her five children and loved them as his own.

As a young man, Jim had been drafted into the army and sent to Vietnam. Assigned to be a forward spotter, he occupied a camouflaged hole in the ground for weeks at a time while spying on the Vietcong as they moved through that part of the jungle. Fear was a constant companion—if discovered, he would have been tortured and killed.

In spite of all this, Jim was a kind and gentle man, smart and well-respected by coworkers and patients alike. A quirky sense of humor accompanied his easy laugh. He quickly became my friend as well as colleague in this stressful professional setting.

When Jim got burned out after many years of practicing direct patient care, he transferred to the information technology department, where he could engage his "techie" side. I wondered about his choice, but he studied hard, and when he got the job, we rejoiced with him.

I lost track of him a few months later, but another coworker kept in touch. Jane was the first to tell me about Jim's diagnosis of colon cancer. She also told me his ominous family history: Jim's father had died of the disease while in his early fifties. Jim was only slightly older than that now.

The doctors jumped into action. Aggressive treatment resulted in a period of remission, but the cancer returned within a couple of years. Jim courageously reengaged the battle, enduring more surgery, radiation, and chemotherapy over the next three years.

Tumors eventually invaded his lungs, leaving him fighting for breath. Finally, only morphine offered relief. How much longer could his battered body last?

Jane and I understood that his time on earth was dwindling. We invited Jim to lunch—our treat—at Arby's, his favorite restaurant. He spent time reminiscing about his life and relationships. Then he showed us pictures of his beloved bichon frise, relieved he had found someone to adopt his doggy friend when the time came.

The conversation inevitably turned to his condition.

"There's really not that much pain," he said. "Sleeping a lot lately. The tightness in my chest is the worst part. The morphine keeps me from feeling like I'm suffocating, but I have to be really careful."

It was a complex balancing act: excessive sleepiness or a struggle to breathe. An accidental overdose would be fatal, forcing him into a coma and respiratory arrest. As long as he was cautious, he said, life wasn't too bad.

But facing his impending death—that was another story. Jim was afraid to die, afraid to face the God who "hated" him. He freely admitted it. Nothing we said made any difference.

Our friend's health deteriorated over the following months, leaving him housebound and alone. Jane and the new "doggy mom" were the only ones he allowed to visit him at home.

Jim weighed heavily on my mind that Saturday evening at Bible study. My heart ached. My friend just couldn't die believing that God hated him! I closed my eyes in prayer along with the other participants. "Please, God," I whispered desperately, "do something!"

The entire atmosphere shifted. My soul became alerted to the unexpected and nonhuman presence I felt standing directly in front of me.

It was not exuding power or love or peace or any kind of threat. It was just . . . there.

Silent.

Motionless.

My eyes stayed closed to prevent any distraction. Concentration narrowed to pinpoint focus as I whispered, "Who are you?"

Curiosity, not fear, moved me. Then comprehension dawned. This was an angel! I'd never encountered one before, nor have I since, but that's what it was. It was the only conclusion that made sense.

My next question: "What do you want?"

I recognized it as a messenger awaiting directions. What should I do? I certainly didn't want to waste such an incredible opportunity!

All right, think, I told myself. What had been uppermost in my mind? Jim and his condition.

That was it!

"Go to my friend Jim, and tell him about God's love." Anxiety flared. Was I doing the right thing? With sudden assurance, I repeated the command more confidently.

I felt the angel zoom off to my right—the direction of Jim's house.

The Bible study continued as I sat there dumbfounded. After the meeting ended, the study leader approached me. "I was watching you while we prayed. What happened? You looked kind of stunned." After I told her what I had felt and done, she agreed with my conclusion: angelic encounter.

The entire event had lasted only a minute or two.

My worry about Jim melted away. Even though I couldn't visit him, someone else could. Someone silent and unseen, but who could still speak to his heart.

Jim's funeral took place only three weeks later. When I saw his picture at the closed-casket service, any residual doubt evaporated. I knew my friend had died at peace. All was well.

Heaven and earth had intersected at this crucial juncture. An angel had come to me and then taken the words of Jesus' love to a dying man who thought God hated him.

That messenger brought peace to us both. Jim received God's love before he died.

And me? Well, I grew up in a church that was fond of emphasizing our individual responsibilities. We were expected to see people converted and keep track of our successes. "You could be the only Bible they ever read," was an oft-spoken phrase. I lived in dread of God's anger at my failures.

Jim and I had been more alike than I thought.

But a messenger angel showing up and waiting patiently for me to figure out what to do helped me understand just how very much God cares about all that concerns me. His love is perfect; I don't have to be.

Message received.

An Angel with God's Healing

INGRID SHELTON

"Mom's in the hospital. Kidney failure," my sister relayed over the phone.

"Oh dear, how is she?" I asked, shocked at this unexpected news.

"Doctors think it's quite serious." I could tell she was choking back tears.

I glanced at the clock. "It's almost ten. Do you think I should come right now or in the morning?"

"It's a long drive. Better come tomorrow," my sister advised. "I'll stay with her as long as I can."

"I think you're right. I'll leave first thing in the morning. Keep me informed if she gets worse," I said.

After I hung up, I sat for a moment in stunned silence. Should I really wait until tomorrow or go now? I agonized. My husband was watching the late news in the living room, but he would need to stay home with our young daughter, who was already asleep. It would take me an hour to get to the city hospital, and at that time the hospital staff might not even allow me to visit.

Yet, I felt so restless. I had to do something. Perhaps I should go anyway. I was sure I wouldn't be able to sleep for worrying about Mom. She had suffered from kidney problems for several years already, but it had never been that serious. But now . . . . would she survive? The thought gripped me like cement and wouldn't let me rest.

Pray! The thought catapulted into my mind and filled my soul. I believed in prayer, but I had never prayed seriously about a health problem for anyone. But didn't the Bible admonish us to pray for everything? Just then a Bible verse popped into my mind: "Do not be anxious about anything, but in every situation, by prayer and petition, with thanksgiving, present your requests to God. And the peace of God, which transcends all understanding, will guard your hearts and your minds in Christ Jesus" (Philippians 4:6–7).

Praying for her would be the best way to help Mom, I decided. I headed to the bathroom to be alone and looked for a good place to pray. Should I just sit down on the toilet seat and pray? No. I had serious matters to attend to with the Lord, and somehow I felt that kneeling would be the best way to keep focused.

"Lord," I began as I knelt beside the bathtub, "please look after Mom. Keep her alive. Grant her many more years." I hardly noticed the minutes ticking by. The burden for Mom just wouldn't leave my heart, so I kept praying, agonizing, pleading with God to restore Mom to health.

Suddenly my soul felt light. The burden had lifted. I got up from my knees. Somehow, I knew the Lord had heard my prayer. When I finally got into bed, I fell asleep almost instantly.

The next morning, I awoke early and kissed my husband good-bye when he left for work. After I dropped off my daughter at school, I drove to the hospital, wondering how I would find Mom. As I entered her room, Mom was propped up against a pillow, happy to see me. I sat next to her bed and asked how she felt.

"I feel great." Mom looked at me intently. "But I have something to tell you." Mom could hardly contain her joy. "Late last night I saw an angel standing beside my bed. Her long gown shimmered like crystal, and her large wings were folded. This graceful angel stood there for a few minutes, not saying a word but just moving from the bottom of the bed to the top." She paused to wipe away a tear, then continued, "Suddenly I felt better. No pain and no discomfort. I knew I was well again. And I knew the angel had come because you were praying for me."

"Oh, Mom." I bent down to hug her. "That's wonderful. I'm so glad you saw that angel. I'm sure God sent the angel to make you all better, to heal you."

Mom nodded. "I was wide awake when the angel came, and I could hardly keep my eyes off her. She brought such peace to my heart."

"Mom, that's the best news you could have given me. I am so happy about it."

Mom never had any problem with her kidneys again. The healing was complete and lasted throughout the rest of her life.

"Thank you, Lord, for sending an angel to heal Mom," I whispered on my way home. "Thank you for showing us that your heavenly messengers are always there to help and to heal us."

I learned that praying for others is God's will for us, as Galatians 6:2 says, "Carry each other's burdens, and in this way you will fulfill the law of Christ." I learned that God has many different ways of healing people, but sending a real live angel in answer to prayer was a gift from God that Mom and I could never forget.

The Light Exposing Evil

SHARON PADGETT CAMPBELL
WITH CAROLYN ROTH BARNUM

A leather glove scraped my throat and threw back my covers. A figure stood a few inches from my bed. Heart racing, I sat up.

The figure swayed, his hands moving behind his back, his body twisting just enough so I could see he held something shiny.

A knife or a gun? Was he going to kill me?

That summer my family had moved across town into a newly built parsonage next to the church my father pastored. It was exciting to think about going into ninth grade and making new friends. Our church had an active youth group, and several kids joined that summer.

Keith was one of them.

"There's a new boy in our youth group," I told Mom. "He's cute, funny, and tall with dark, curly hair."

"Cute *and* tall," she teased.

"Mom . . . I really like him, and he likes me." My mother smiled her approval.

Her smile would disappear in the months ahead.

Keith and I were inseparable during the summer. By the time school started, we were a couple. Along with my brother Jimmy and his friend Chad, Keith and I walked to and from school every day, laughing and talking.

Early in October Keith announced, "My parents are inviting our youth group to a Halloween party in our backyard. They will decorate and provide the food. All we have to do is plan the games."

As the night of the party approached, some of the kids began to tease me. "Keith is going to kiss you," they said. "You know he will."

Their plan was to leave the backyard and board the church bus as soon as the party ended. That would give Keith his chance. They were sure he wouldn't kiss me in front of all of them. They were right. As soon as they left, Keith kissed me. My very first kiss.

Keith walked me to the bus. When the kids saw the look on my face, they knew their plan had succeeded.

I never suspected that his kiss on that night of make-believe ghosts and goblins would lead to a nightmare I would live with the rest of my life.

By the middle of November, Keith's fun-loving mood changed. He grew sullen. He resented Jimmy and Chad walking with us. Possessive and controlling, he expected me to exclude everyone, including my family.

"You're *my* girlfriend," Keith yelled. "Don't forget it. You're going to regret it if you do."

I resented his attitude and was frightened at the same time.

I stopped seeing Keith and spent time with other friends, including Chad. One afternoon I waited for Chad to finish football practice. Keith waited, too. As Chad and I walked home holding hands, Keith walked with us.

He suddenly turned toward me and snarled, "I'm warning you, Sharon. If we don't go back to the way we were, I'm going to kill you."

"Yeah, yeah," Chad mocked. "Get lost. Sharon is through with you. Leave her alone."

It wasn't the first time Keith had said such things. It was his way of getting attention. I was sure he would tire of trying to change my mind. Chad and I walked off, ignoring him.

Keith would soon prove he had no intention of letting us or anyone else dismiss him so lightly.

Two weeks later, after my family's traditional Thanksgiving dinner, everyone in our family except Jimmy attended the football game held between two local teams. Not feeling well, Jimmy stayed home and was lying on the couch in the family room when Keith walked in. He was furious when Jimmy said I was at the game with Chad. He stomped out of the room and went into the kitchen.

It wasn't unusual that Keith had walked into our house and made himself at home. He'd been part of my family since he and I had started seeing each other. Unaware of Keith's recent behavior, my parents were still fond of him.

While Keith rummaged in the kitchen, Jimmy dozed off. He woke upon hearing Mom's electric knife sharpener. He looked up as Keith came out of the kitchen with the knife he'd sharpened. It was the same large knife Keith often carried when he was with guys from school.

"See this knife?" he shouted at Jimmy. "I'm gonna kill Sharon with it tonight!"

Jimmy stared at Keith. Knowing Keith's mood swings, he passed it off as another of Keith's idle threats. "Keith, you're making my headache worse. Go home and take your stupid knife with you."

Instead of leaving, Keith went into my parents' bedroom. He knew Dad kept a broken shotgun in their closet. He checked to make sure it was disabled. He picked up Jimmy's bow and arrow, took them into the family room, and pointed them at Jimmy. Just then Chad and I arrived. Chad took the bow and arrow away from Keith and echoed Jimmy's stern suggestion that Keith leave. He stormed out.

Chad stayed with us until my parents returned. Exhausted from all the holiday activities, we went to bed early.

I had just fallen asleep when something rough scraped across my throat. The room was dark. I could barely make out the shape of something or someone standing by my bed. My heart raced. I sat up.

The figure swayed from side to side. At first I could distinguish only a shape. It leaned toward me, revealing something in its hand. A gun? A knife? I cried out, "Who are you? Why are you here?"

It made no reply but continued swaying back and forth, moving closer. I kept talking, hoping to distract it. "If you want money, my purse is on my dresser. I don't have much, but take what there is and leave." It took another step toward me.

Did this "thing" plan to kill me?

I glanced away, frantic to find a way to escape. I saw none. In desperation I silently prayed, *God, help me. I don't want to die.*

A light suddenly appeared, revealing the figure. It was Keith!

Stay calm, God whispered to my spirit. *Don't let him know you recognize him.*

At that moment, Keith raised his hand. A silver knife blade, poised high, reflected the light in the darkness. Instinctively I lifted my hands to protect my head. I felt the knife hit me again and again. Screaming, I lost track of how many times it struck.

Hearing my screams, my parents dashed out of their room. Dad saw my open door and glimpsed a figure running through the living room and kitchen and into the night. Unable to catch the person, he returned to the house and called the police.

Mom ran into my room, turned on the light, and saw the blood oozing down my head and face. She rushed me into the bathroom. She began washing the blood out of my hair and off my hands, treating my wounds.

"It's a miracle these aren't worse," Mom said on the verge of tears. "I'm so grateful, but I don't understand how it's possible. You were stabbed multiple times, yet the cuts are not deep."

Mom's assurance that my wounds were not life threatening calmed me, although I was still shaking from my near-death experience. She finished bandaging my hands and helped me change out of my bloodied pajamas. We joined Dad in the kitchen.

"The police will be here any minute," Dad said. Then he held me on his lap like he did when I was a little girl.

"I know who did this, Daddy. It was Keith," I said.

"You need to be sure, honey."

"I'm positive. I could see him even though the room was dark."

The police had arrived and one of them asked, "If it was dark, how could you see the person who attacked you?"

"While I was praying for God to help me, a light appeared behind him. I could see the leather jacket he always wears with the collar turned up. He had a bandana on his face, but it didn't hide his curly hair."

I laid my head back on my dad's shoulder, trembling as I recalled earlier incidents. "Keith has threatened to kill me several times in front of my friends. We just thought he was trying to get attention. When I saw him in my room, I knew he meant it."

The policeman looked skeptical until Jimmy backed up my accusation. "He threatened her again tonight. He even showed me his knife."

The police went to Keith's home and found him pretending to be asleep. His window was partially open. His pants and shoes were covered with burrs from weeds in the adjacent lot.

Keith was in handcuffs when the police brought him by our house. They walked with him to our carport, and we confronted him. He seemed stunned to see I was still alive. He began pleading with me. "Sharon, you know I would never try to kill you. I love you too much. It wasn't me."

I shook a bandaged finger in his face, summoned my courage, and declared, "It *was* you!"

By this time some neighbors had gathered. Just before Keith was put into the police car, he turned and shouted, "One of these days I'll finish what I started!"

Later the police told us Keith admitted he was the one in my room that night. "Not only that," they said, "but he has been in your bedroom every night this week. He took trinkets, pieces of jewelry, items that wouldn't be missed right away. He was obsessed with punishing you for breaking up with him. He fantasized about other ways to harm you—poison, kidnapping, and torture. You're a very lucky girl to be alive. We found the knife, so we have plenty of evidence to convict him even without your eyewitness account."

Seeing our puzzled looks, the policeman continued. "The authorities have some doubts about the sudden appearance of a light that helped you identify him."

"It happened," I said. "God made it happen."

"Keith is also being questioned about a number of other unsolved crimes in the community—auto vandalism, arson, and theft. We've had our eye on him for some time, and we're convinced he's our guy."

My father attended Keith's trial. The prosecution said circumstantial evidence and Keith's own words that night proved he came to my room intending to kill me. In addition, during cross-examination, Keith became angry and shouted, "I would have succeeded, except someone came in the room holding a bright light. Whoever it was turned my hand so only the handle struck, not the knife blade."

I shuddered when I heard this, knowing that with scars on my head and hands from the sharp handle, I would not have survived if the blows had been made with the knife blade.

"You were right, honey," Daddy said. "God did protect you."

Years later I told my grown children about the incident. My son looked at me with tears in his eyes. "Mom, that light behind Keith was God's angel. It allowed you to identify Keith and kept him from stabbing you with the knife blade."

More than fifty years later my brush with death still affects me. I am always aware, sometimes wary, of my surroundings. Yet I am also aware God is surrounding me with His love at all times.

I am a miracle. I live today only because God sent a light into the darkness when I needed it. Without that light, I could not have identified the figure as Keith. It reminds me that God sent His Son, Jesus, to be our light in the darkness. Without faith in Him, we cannot see.

I Saw Jesus Weeping

Judith Vander Wege

"Where's the abundant life you promised me in John 10:10?" I asked God. I felt abandoned by God because He hadn't healed my marriage, and I felt I couldn't trust Him anymore.

Desperate for love, I became involved in an adulterous relationship and told my husband we needed to get a divorce. His obvious relief did not help me feel better.

After the divorce in July 1981, the grief and guilt nearly crushed me. As a Christian, I knew adultery was wrong. Could I have any hope to fit into God's plan for my life again?

I married my boyfriend as soon as I could after the divorce, but the relationship was stressful because he didn't have a job and soon went back to his partying lifestyle. The relationship was a big disappointment since I couldn't trust him or depend on him. And I continued to feel guilty for getting involved with him. A friend told me, "Judy, you're dragging Christ's name in the mud!"

I knew she was right, but I didn't feel capable of doing anything differently. I felt like I'd fallen into a slimy pit and couldn't get out.

One day, I read words in Isaiah that gripped my heart: "This is a people robbed and plundered . . . trapped in holes and hidden in prisons; they have become a prey with none to rescue, a spoil with none to say, 'Restore!'" (42:22 RSV).

Those words describe me! I thought. As I reread them, I began to think, *Perhaps the Lord does understand and care how I feel!* As I read the rest of Isaiah, I grew to love it as it showed me a merciful God who longs to rescue us from Satan's traps and draw us into His heart.

I joined a little church, appropriately named Hope, and the congregants ministered the love of God to me, praying for me and speaking the Word of God into my soul. One of my new friends called herself my sister and gave me much good advice. She told me of a seminar that she thought would help me. I attended this seminar, and I learned true repentance is seeing your heart as God sees it—when your heart breaks at what breaks God's heart. Then I realized that adultery was not my only sin. I also displayed judgmental attitudes, resentment, bitterness, selfishness, pride, idolatry, and rebellion.

Chapter 1 of Isaiah showed me God's heart, which was broken by His rebellious children—including me. I should have known I could trust Him, for I'd been God's child for nearly three decades. But instead of trusting Him, I'd rebelled and gone my own way. Like Eve in the Garden of Eden, I'd picked forbidden fruit. I was injured, afflicted, and desolate (Isaiah 1:5, 7) because of my own rebellion.

As I thought of God's heart breaking over my sinful attitudes and deeds, my heart broke. I repented fully. I wanted a restored relationship with my Lord and heavenly Father more than anything else. I learned that God loved me in spite of my sin, and like Isaiah says, He was calling me back to himself. I was astounded by His mercy.

Isaiah's name means "salvation is of the Lord." This prophet gave hope of salvation and restoration to the people of Judah for sixty years. "'Come now, and let us reason together,' says the Lord. 'Though your sins are like scarlet, they shall be as white as snow; though they are red like crimson, they shall be as wool. If you are willing and obedient, you shall eat the good of the land'" (Isaiah 1:18–19 NKJV). This sounds like the Lord loves to forgive. He longs for us to return to Him so He can bless us. This gave me hope.

Isaiah told in chapter 6 of a vision God had given him. It must have transformed Isaiah's life as well as commissioned him for the service of being a prophet.

God gave me a vision, too, during a painful and scary incident. That transforming vision enabled me to trust Him better. One night in 1984, my second husband came home at two in the morning, stoned and drunk, as usual. He woke me up and insisted I go to the store and get him some cigarettes. I'd previously done whatever he asked, but the people at Al-Anon said we needed to quit being enablers. I'd prayed that God would guide me and help me not enable him to continue his addictions. I didn't approve of smoking, and I didn't think I should help him do something that was bad for his health. Besides, I considered it a ridiculous request at two in the morning.

"No," I said.

He acted like he didn't believe me.

"I jus' need some cig'rettes and my truck's outa gas. You take your car and go get me some."

"No," I said again, quite firmly.

He "explained" again, then clenched both hands around my neck. When I still refused to do what he wanted, he squeezed tighter. It hurt, but I managed to get a finger under his hands so I could breathe and talk.

"If you kill me, I'll go to heaven, but you'll have it on your conscience all your life," I told him. Then I silently prayed. After a few moments, he rolled over and sank into a drunken stupor.

As I lay there in the darkness with my neck aching, in the midst of my heartaches and fears, I cried out to Jesus, "Do you want me to hurt like this?"

I saw Jesus sitting nearby, weeping as if His heart would break. He shook His head and said, "No! No, I don't want you to hurt like that. I love you!"

Confused, I wondered why He didn't take me out of my situation. But I believed Him.

He loves me! He doesn't want me to hurt. Then the thought occurred to me, *He looks like He's waiting for me to do something. What is it?*

Trembling, I quietly got up, hoping my husband wouldn't wake up. I called a friend who was a social worker. I told him what had happened, and he agreed to stay at our house the rest of the night to make sure I was safe. I went to the guest room and tried to sleep. My friend tried to talk sense to my husband in the morning.

Then I called our pastor, and he sent a Christian couple over to talk with us. When my husband saw the marks on my neck, he agreed to weekly counseling and to abstain from using alcohol and marijuana. He seemed sober for the next few weeks, so I thought maybe the choking incident was resulting in some good. He'd never been sober that long before.

Throughout this time, my vision of Jesus weeping over me gave me comfort. I believed He loved me. Believing Jesus loved me that much gave me the courage to trust Him completely, to place my life in His hands. Determined to obey Him, I asked Jesus Christ to take back the throne of my heart. I had let my emotions rule me, but now I knew I needed to leave that idolatry behind and let Jesus rule me.

I kept praying that my husband's heart and life would change, too, but I didn't see evidence of that. The choking incident happened two years after we married. Before and after, I felt a lot of confusion about how to deal with my husband's behavior and his lack of contribution to our finances. Members of the Al-Anon group said, "Don't enable your spouse's addictions," yet I was trying to show him Christ-like love, and I couldn't figure out how to do that without enabling him.

A few weeks after the choking incident and during the weekly counseling, I found out my husband had continued to smoke marijuana daily. Since he was not staying sober, I had a feeling of impending doom. The church offered to pay for him to go to Teen Challenge, which helps people recover from alcoholism and addictions, but he refused. Problems related to his addictions escalated until I felt I must choose either to stay on a conveyor belt to destruction or to let God rescue me.

My pastor said, "We can't change him, but we can help you."

So the church paid for me to get counseling. At the third session with a Christian psychiatrist, after I'd told him about the latest problem, he said, "Let's pray." After we prayed together, the psychiatrist said, "I saw a vision of your husband coming after you with a knife, and I was standing between. Pray more about this and talk to your pastor before you decide for sure, but I think you should consider separating."

I did as he recommended. My pastor and an elder changed the locks on my mobile home and took my husband's belongings to him.

He called me a few times after that, trying to manipulate me into letting him back into my home. But I felt I just couldn't handle life with him anymore. I kept having nightmares. He'd already had seven "dramatic turnarounds" in the three years we'd been together. I knew now I couldn't save him. After three years of trying to be a vehicle God could use to bring my husband into His kingdom, I gave up, divorcing him. Of course, I felt like a failure all over again.

One thing he said helped me feel better: "God sent me an angel to show me the way, but I wouldn't listen," thus admitting his fault. I heard that he later did go to Teen Challenge but wouldn't follow the rules and was asked to leave.

A couple of Scriptures reinforced God's message of love to me. One was, "'I will come to you and fulfill my good promise to bring you back. . . . For I know the plans I have for you,' declares the Lord, 'plans to prosper you and not to harm you, plans to give you hope and a future'" (Jeremiah 29:10–11).

The other Scripture had been meaningful to me from childhood: "And we know that in all things God works for the good of those who love him, who have been called according to his purpose" (Romans 8:28).

God doesn't force us to fit into His good plans. He lets us choose whether to follow Him or not. Moses said: "I have set before you life and death, blessings and curses. Now choose life, so that you and your children may live and that you may love the Lord your God, listen to his voice, and hold fast to him. For the Lord is your life" (Deuteronomy 30:19–20).

I thank God for the vision that helped convince me of His deep love for me and helped me trust Him and choose to live submitted to Him.

Hallway of Heavenly Light

Paul F. Bauer

Cruising down the busy city street, the white patrol car with a large police shield adhered to each front door glistened in the late afternoon sunshine. Inside Joey Ballantine and Michelle Cabrera debated who had higher scores at the police shooting range.

"I can outshoot you any day, and you know it," proclaimed Cabrera, a slender, dark-haired veteran with twelve years on the force. Her father, a retired police detective, had made sure all of his four children could shoot a gun well.

"Really?" questioned Ballantine, a medium-framed man of average height with light-brown hair and eight years of police experience. Unlike his patrol partner, shooting was something he first learned to do in the police academy.

Breaking up the debate, a female voice over the police radio requested, "Available unit in the south end respond to 1411 Chambers Street, apartment number thirty-seven, report of possible 10-21." (A 10-21 refers to domestic violence.)

Sitting in the passenger's seat because she was the senior officer and drove enough shuffling her three kids around town, Cabrera grabbed the radio mic. "Unit S-15 is en route," she announced as she flipped the overheard light bar and siren on from the console between the front seats.

The police dispatcher returned, "Be advised the address has priors on record."

Taking the turn onto Fourteenth Street toward Chambers fast enough to squeal the tires, Ballantine remarked, "Oh yeah, we have been there before, Michelle. Remember that guy Ray who could never pass the psychological exam for cops?"

"Is he that goofy little guy?" she asked as the patrol car cut across two lanes of Fourteenth and onto Chambers.

"Correct. He and his wife had an argument, but we saw no physical harm and she wouldn't sign a complaint against him," Joey recounted.

Michelle added, "Yes, and she refused to go to Hope Home for Abused and Battered Women."

The late model patrol car screeched to a stop in front of 1411 Chambers Street. When they were first built, the apartments were considered affordable, low-cost housing. Now, years later, most people just referred to them as the Projects, a collection of rundown buildings in a depressed part of the south side of the city.

"Dispatch, unit S-15 off at 1411 Chambers and heading to the third floor in the left hallway, number thirty-seven," Michelle radioed in as they exited the patrol car.

"10-4. Due to priors, unit S-18 is responding as backup." Dispatch reminded them of the new mandatory policy that had been put in place since so many police officers were injured in the city the previous year on repeat domestic violence calls.

Briskly, Ballantine and Cabrera walked through the double glass doors of the ten-story, plain red-brick building. Once the jewel of urban renewal in the city, all the complex's doorways used to have locked entries. Now the metal door housing only contained an empty hole where the lock cylinder once fit. The locks had long since been punched out and never replaced, and now anyone could access the building. Up the old, dirty staircase they climbed. At the second-floor landing, a middle-aged woman with brown, greasy hair said in a hushed voice, "Bad before but never this bad. I heard banging on the floor above." And she pointed up toward unit number thirty-seven.

Both officers nodded and headed up the steps in silence. On the third floor, off to the left in an enclosed hallway, was number thirty-seven, the last door on the right. Banging hard on the door, they each tactically stood to one side of the door and announced in unison, "Police department."

A short white man in unkempt clothes and a buzz cut pulled open the door several inches with the chain lock in place.

"Remember me? We talked about job options for you last month?" Joey asked.

"Oh yeah," the man said as he closed the door to unlock it. Joey and Michelle exchanged looks.

The door opened just enough for both cops to see the head of a woman who was lying unconscious on the floor behind the man. It distracted them just long enough for the man, Ray, to bring his handgun upward and fire a round, which struck Joey in the left leg, causing him to bend sideways and catch the next shot in the upper right side of his neck. This pushed him back against the hallway wall opposite the doorway. As he slid down to the floor, his right hand instinctively searched for his holstered weapon.

Suddenly, several loud explosions sent up puffs of grayish-white smoke on his right. Michelle had responded to Ray's horrific act in a split second, firing two rounds from her 9 mm into Ray's chest, effectively stopping the violent assault. Ray's body slapped the bare floor of his apartment as Joey's crumpled over, leaning against the now bloodstained hallway wall.

Billy, a cop from unit S-18, charged down the hallway toward Michelle.

"Secure the weapon, and check the woman," Michelle commanded.

"Joey!" she cried, rushing to his side while fumbling for her radio. "1011 dispatch—shots fired—officer down—we need EMS for the officer and two others. Perpetrator in custody."

As she dropped on her knees at Joey's side, he saw a bright light coming up behind her in the hallway. Desperately Cabrera tried to stop the blood from Joey's neck with her hands, pressing one on top of the other against the bullet wound.

"Dear Lord in heaven, we need your help right now with Joey," she prayed.

"Use this, Michelle," shouted Billy as he threw a kitchen towel from the apartment toward her.

As Joey strained to move his neck, he saw Michelle silhouetted by a bright light filling the hallway. Its rays extended beyond Michelle's body and darted across the dirty walls, beckoning to him. "Come and find rest for your weary soul," came a gentle whisper softly flowing down the hallway.

Michelle pressed the towel firmly against his bleeding neck and rocked back and forth, saying a barely audible prayer.

"What is happening?" Joey asked as he saw fast, fluttering motions behind her like translucent wings.

"Shut up and don't try to talk, Joey," she begged, worried about the amount of blood that had soaked into his shirt and right pant leg.

"Uh, you're an angel. That's why you're fluttering," Joey whispered, feeling the slight breeze of the angel's graceful wings across his face.

"What did he say?" asked Billy, leaning toward them by the apartment doorway. "Hang in there, Joey," he yelled, concerned their brother officer was close to passing into the place where angels fly.

The screaming voice of his coworker pulled Joey back to this side of life.

"Yeah," he coughed out with spit and blood, looking up at the husky cop.

Joey shivered; the cold was bone deep. Pins and needles tingled his skin. He felt faint, like he was going to throw up.

"No, take me down the hallway of light, angel," he begged as his eyes focused on Michelle.

Billy and Michelle glanced at one another, puzzled and worried.

A wry smile reflected Joey's relief as he saw supernatural shapes down the hallway. He saw two more angels descend at his end of the enclosed hallway.

"Yes!" he gurgled through saliva and mucus.

One angel flew past him and hovered near his left leg. The other angel had the form of an older black man. He had short gray hair and a clean-shaven baby face, and he wore wire-rimmed glasses and an EMS uniform.

"You are going to be just fine," Joey heard him declare as he and Michelle changed places with a loud fluttering of wings and blast of air.

Joey's heart jumped with excitement at the remarkable sight in the center of the hallway. He hadn't even noticed that the EMS angels had brought his transport to eternal peace and floated it down next to him. A tubular metal chariot with a bright-red bed. Lying on it was a green bottle of oxygen and a clear mask that Joey figured he would need for the transition "up there."

"Who are you calling?" a dismayed Billy questioned Michelle, who had backed down the hallway.

"My church prayer chain," she said, holding her phone with bloodied fingers.

"You are calling right now?" Billy inquired.

"Yeah," she answered. "If we don't get people praying for Joey right now, we will lose him, Billy." Tears fell from her eyes.

The second angel, in the form of a young Asian man with long dark hair pulled back in a ponytail, tugged at Joey's leg, pulling him back to earth.

"Hey, get me back . . ." Joey didn't have strength to complete his demand that the young medic get him back to the hallway of light.

"This bullet wound here is a clean in and out," Tommy Kim, the young medic, reported to Samuel Jeffers, the older medic, who said something in return that Joey didn't hear. He was losing consciousness.

Yes, back to the hallway of light. Joey felt warm and comfy all over.

"We are going to get you up now, Joey," said Samuel, shaking while his wings picked up speed. Joey smiled.

"Here we go," he said, lifting Joey effortlessly upward and down the hallway of lights.

"Please get the calls going out to all the prayer warriors right now!" he heard Michelle say into her phone as he glided past her in the hallway.

Suddenly, Joey saw bright lights, but not the same kind of bright. They were not nearly as bright as the hallway and emitted a harsher light.

"What happened?" he heard his gravelly voice ask through a painful throat. He squinted at the bright light that he now recognized as the fluorescent lights of a hospital ceiling. Joey felt the coldness in his body all the way down to his feet, telling him he was no longer in the warm hallway of light.

"You really gave everybody a scare, Joey. A lot of people were praying for you, and God answered; you are alive, and I think your prognosis for a full recovery is very good."

Joey's neck was restricted from movement by dressings. He could only glance toward the tall, lean man dressed in scrubs with a name and "MD" written on it, standing on his left. Lightly squeezing Joey's left shoulder with a firm hand, the thin doctor with hairy arms advised, "Get some rest, Joey; plenty of folks want to visit with you later!"

The group shuffled out of the room, some looking back and nodding at Joey. He began to grasp that he had hovered between two worlds. He desired to be in the hallway of light to heaven. However, all these medical folks and Michelle's prayer warriors here desired to keep him on earth. God heard their prayers and made the decision: Joey would stay on earth for quite a while longer.

Making peace with his rescinded chariot trip, Joey figured God must have things for him to do down here yet. Thoughtfully replaying the last day in his mind, he considered what changes he would make in his extended life. Joey decided the most powerful change he would make would be to pray for others in need. He couldn't wait to tell Michelle and to thank her for those prayers. Laughing to himself, he wondered if anyone would ever believe his experience in the hallway of lights and how close he came to heaven.

A Warm, Enveloping Glow

Jan Apilado

On a cold Sunday in January as worship began, my three children and I filed into the pew at church. A dear widow, Florence, who sat in front of us, turned and asked, "Where's Corky?"

"In Los Angeles for business," I whispered.

"I must tell you, the Lord woke me up at three this morning. He put your husband's face in front of me and told me to pray. I stayed up the rest of the night praying for him. He seemed in trouble," she whispered.

Oh no! I thought. *What on earth is going on?*

Our dear Florence was a sweet woman who walked closely with our Lord. After her words, I was so concerned for my husband that it was difficult to concentrate on the worship. During the pastor's message, I could only think of Florence's words. My peace and joy were gone.

This was before cell phones were available, and none of the companies we represented would answer their phones until

Monday morning, so I had no way to contact my husband until then. We had no idea where he was staying. I reminded the children, and myself, that praying for Daddy and trusting the Lord were the only things we could do. I told them we would have to wait and that Daddy would call us.

This had all begun over three months earlier when a young man participating in an evangelism movement called us. It was a September afternoon, and I answered the phone call from a young seminary student who introduced himself as Chuck. His first question was, "Are you certain you are saved?"

Yes, I had accepted Jesus as a young teen, I explained, but my husband had not. But I had drawn away from the Lord and had no church affiliation. Over the phone, this young man helped me to reconfirm my faith in our Lord Jesus. He prayed with me, then asked about my husband's schedule. Corky was out selling that day. So Chuck suggested that he and his wife, Isaura, come visit on Wednesday night to meet with my husband. I agreed that would be fine.

After Corky arrived home that evening, I mentioned that I had rededicated my life to Jesus over the phone that day. He seemed glad for me. But when I told him about Chuck coming over on Wednesday evening to meet with him, he responded, "Well, don't expect me to be here!"

"Okay," I said.

By Wednesday night, Corky had forgotten about Chuck's visit. When he and his wife arrived, I invited them in. Corky, always a good host, joined them in the living room, while I made sure our kids were busy in their rooms. Then I joined the adults.

Chuck, a warm and easygoing guy, was an instant friend. Corky enjoyed Chuck and Isaura's company so much that he invited them to join us for Sunday dinner after their church service. Chuck and Isaura gladly accepted. They attended a church less than two blocks from our home.

That was the first of many Sunday dinners we shared with them. About a month later, Chuck and Isaura brought along a seminary friend named Meije, who came from Haiti. Meije told us about his amazing salvation experience during a life-or-death struggle. In Haiti, he had been a commercial fisherman. He admitted that he'd been a hard-drinking, wild youth, believing that he was indestructible. Then came the day when he and the crew were caught in a terrific storm and their boat was demolished. Meije, fighting huge waves with many sharks circling him, knew death was near. At that moment, he called out to God. He promised that if he was saved from this, he would dedicate his whole life to serving the Lord. So here he was in our living room, fulfilling a part of his promise.

Both Chuck and Meije faithfully and gently presented Jesus' sacrifice for Corky each time they visited. Even as they both stressed Corky's need to repent and be saved, Corky continued to resist making any commitment. Yet he kept inviting them to Sunday dinner. He enjoyed their friendship but refused their invitation to accept Jesus as his Savior.

Over the course of more than three months, this pattern continued. During that time, the children and I had begun attending their church services on most Sundays. Yet Corky refused to join us. By this time, our seminary students feared that Corky would be eternally lost. Both Chuck and Meije were discouraged. Their final effort was to plead with God over Corky's stubborn refusal to accept that he needed a savior. They shared with me that their last-resort prayer had been, "Lord, we've done all we can. We've said all that you would have us say. We're turning Corky over to you. We don't know what else to do. Lord, we place him in your hands now."

So immediately after the service that Sunday, after Florence told me about her 3:00 a.m. wake-up call, I gathered the children, thanked her, and headed for home, hoping for a phone call from Corky.

Meanwhile in Los Angeles on the Saturday night just before Florence's vision, Corky met with two owners of a company we represented in the Pacific Northwest. To save the hotel expense, one of the owners invited Corky to his home. Corky didn't know that both of these men were wild and heavy drinkers. They expected Corky to join them in their party mode. He appeased them for a while but knew when to stop. As the night went on, they became more out of control.

Near midnight, Corky suddenly felt a cold and evil presence with them in the living room of that house where he was to spend the night. He watched a man who was standing on the hearth. Fear and darkness spread through Corky, and as he studied the man, he said, "You look like the devil!"

With a sneer, the man retorted, "I am the devil!"

Corky could not get out of that house fast enough! He dashed through the front door and zoomed down the sidewalk just as fast as he could run. He heard one of the men yelling after him, "Don't go out there!"

He kept running, not caring that he was leaving all of his luggage and his briefcase behind. He just knew he had to get out of there.

After running several blocks, Corky spotted a taxi and hailed it. Not knowing where to go, he decided the airport was a good choice. All airports are surrounded by hotels. After the driver dropped him off at a hotel, he told the desk clerk that he just wanted a small, secure room. As it turned out, the only available room was a penthouse suite. So, without extra clothes or even a toothbrush, he tried to settle himself into this suite and make some sense of all that he had just experienced. Quite some time passed before his pulse slowed down and he could begin to think somewhat rationally again. As he began to feel a bit less tense, he also began to focus on how he could get back his belongings without stepping into that house again. Being exhausted, he decided he would worry about that in the morning.

As he began to relax, he noticed that his room began to reflect a slowly creeping, soft, warm glow. With each moment, the glow became brighter until his room was as brilliant as the noonday sun. By the warmth, love, and peace he felt, he knew the presence of Jesus was in that room with him. He felt the love of Jesus pouring over him. He dropped to his knees, sobbing, and asked for God's mercy and forgiveness. He said he had never felt so loved as he did in that moment of being in the Lord's presence. It was 3:00 a.m.

After a few hours of rest, Corky phoned a friend who lived near LA. He told him the situation and insisted that he would not enter that house again. Our friend was more than willing to help out and was a tall man who definitely exhibited a don't-mess-with-me attitude.

Corky gave him the address and described his belongings, and our big friend took care of the issue. He then drove Corky to the airport. Corky was on the next flight home. Needless to say, we ceased all business transactions with that company.

So our gracious Lord wakened dear Florence at 3:00 a.m. to pray, and His light shone upon Corky at that same moment. Corky's frightening night proved to him just how much he did need Jesus in his life. This was immediately after our seminary friends had fully submitted Corky to God's plan and power.

A few weeks later, another "God moment" occurred. Corky decided he needed to buy a Bible. For a new believer, our pastor had recommended *The Living Bible*. Corky, not yet fully comfortable with the label of "Christian," carefully drove to a small Bible bookstore. He waited in the car while he looked over the parking lot to make sure he didn't see anyone who knew him. After he decided he was safe, he entered and the clerk showed him to the Bible area. As he was searching the shelves, he heard the bell ring, announcing another customer. Lo and behold, it was Chuck! Walking directly to Corky, he said, "Praise the Lord, brother! You're here to buy a Bible!"

Sometime later, Corky left the business world, applied to a seminary, and became a pastor. All because of a 3:00 a.m. wake-up call!

In Another Realm

ELIZABETH GARRETT

Whether it's sweltering hot or bone-chilling cold, in Mississippi, September signals time for football. Some years it's hot and cold in the same week, but when I was a kid, we just wanted to get outside and play regardless of the temperature.

Since no one in our neighborhood had much money, we had to play with whatever we had. If that meant being a girl and playing football, that's what happened.

On one particular afternoon when I was twelve, I could hardly wait to join the neighborhood kids. It was a Friday and warm outside when I ran into the house after school, threw on a pair of shorts, and rounded up the teams. We played in the next-door neighbor's yard, and the hard clay ground served as our football field. Stadium fans included neighborhood children who weren't picked for the teams, although they didn't seem to mind being spectators. They lined the "field" with lawn chairs so they could cheer for their favorite players.

"One, two, three, hike," my friend Elinda shouted. Poised for a big play, I darted to catch the ball. Instead, her brother Ralphie zipped past me, snatched it from in front of my face, and went for the touchdown. Determined to prevent him from scoring, I ran as fast as my stout legs would carry me. Instead of modeling perfect form, I toppled, taking scrawny little Ralphie all the way down.

Clunk! Everything went dark. My five-foot-seven-and-a-half-inch frame sprawled on the ground right on top of Ralphie's tennis shoes. Neighbors told me I created quite a scene as I convulsed on the ground. One of my biggest opponents, Cindy from across the street, ran to grab a wet dishcloth to throw on my face. She claimed she couldn't find a clean washcloth in such a hurry. Parents poured out of houses to see what had happened. One of the dads bravely stuck his finger in my mouth to keep me from swallowing my tongue. I continued convulsing and didn't seem aware.

Desperate for help, my parents gave up on the ambulance and tossed me onto the back seat of our light-blue 1968 Ford Mercury.

During the ride to the hospital, I heard talking but couldn't make out the words. I sensed concern and fear. A few minutes into the ride, I began to see again, though my perspective had changed. I looked down from above the car and saw my dad driving. My mom sat in the passenger's seat, where she kept glancing back to check on me. Wearing white shorts with large pink and blue flowers, I lay on my side across the seat. I could see grass stains on my blue knit sleeveless shirt and my shorts.

Still in a different realm, I explored my new world. My adventurous spirit, typical of a twelve-year-old extrovert, led me to check out everything I could see. I saw a white corridor filled with light. Unsure of where to go next, I looked around and saw several people walk by. I tried talking with them, but they didn't respond. One man in particular, with long brown hair and a beard, approached me. He stretched out his hand and gently touched my arm. His eyes reflected great love and kindness.

"Hello, child," he said. "It's not meant for you to continue down this hallway right now." He knelt and looked into my eyes, reassuring me I would be okay. "You must go back down." He even pointed the way and waved when I arrived.

Upon being reunited with my body, I went in and out of consciousness for some time. I remember the excitement in my mother's voice when my breathing steadied and I muttered sounds. We arrived at the hospital's emergency room, where people scurried around. Between bouts of hysteria, my parents tried to explain what had happened. The attendants put me on a stretcher and wheeled me off for X-rays. I still remember the hard, cold surface. By this time, I could respond to their directions.

"Turn over on your side. Lie still," said the technician. "I know this is uncomfortable. It will only take a minute."

After what seemed like hours, I was wheeled to a double room. The other occupant was a four-year-old girl who had been critically ill off and on since birth. As her mother explained her struggles, my mom and I gasped in horror. In spite of her challenges, the girl was still able to talk, so we spent some time getting acquainted.

When the doctor came to report on my condition, he explained to my mother and me that I had experienced convulsions from a concussion. He said I would be fine, but he wanted to keep me overnight for observation.

When I returned home, my friends and family bombarded me with phone calls, visits, and gifts. My older brother even broke down and showed some emotion. "Lizzy, you could have died," he said, a serious look on his face.

Yes, I could have, but I didn't. I learned several things during that experience. First of all, no matter what happens, there is always someone in much worse condition than you are, so be kind and reach out to them. Second, appreciate the people in your life. We never know when our lives or the lives of our loved ones here on earth will be over. We must appreciate every second. Third, and most important, I now know firsthand that wherever I am or will be, I will never be alone.

I don't know for sure whether or not my kind guide was Jesus. Whoever he was, he acted as a true friend, pouring out his love and respect. I felt such peace. Without reservation, I acted out of complete trust. I have no doubts God sent me a guide to help me safely arrive at my destination . . . and with a new perspective.

A Supernatural Split Second

Judith Victoria Hensley

As a young teacher and Bible study leader, I often took our youth to events outside of our small community. At the time, I owned a massive green station wagon with wood paneling on the sides. Driving it was like maneuvering a small tank. I raised the reading on the odometer significantly with the trips I made from our rural location to town and to youth events and back.

At that time, seat belts were in vehicles, but it was not illegal to drive without them. And there was no legal limit on how many people could cram into a car. My station wagon often served as a youth-trip bus. I could fit three people in the front seat, maybe four. The back seat could easily hold four skinny teens, and sometimes more. On a crazy day, we might even have a couple of people riding way in the back.

I can't remember exactly who or how many were in the car as we traveled back from our outing, but I know the vehicle was loaded. I drove slowly on the curvy mountain roads. The young people were laughing and making a lot of noise, but I tried to keep my attention on the road.

One curve in particular deserved full attention. The road came around a sharp bend and almost immediately through a one-lane tunnel under the railroad track. It was only a couple of car lengths long and was only wide enough for one car to pass through with two or three feet on each side.

Drivers always followed common courtesy and common sense. If two cars were approaching the tunnel, the first one there was allowed to go first while the other driver pulled over on the two-lane road on their side of the tunnel and waited their turn. The system worked well.

On that day, there must have been a stranger in town or someone driving under the influence of something besides common sense. We were already headed into the tunnel when a huge passenger truck approached. When we realized he wasn't going to stop and there was not room enough to pass, all of the kids started screaming. I'm pretty sure I was calling on Jesus to help us.

If the truck didn't stop, we'd hit it head on. I didn't have time to back up and out of the way. There was no room to pull over and get out of his way inside the tunnel. The width of the tunnel and the width of my station wagon and the big truck did not form a balanced equation. There was simply no way to avoid a serious collision.

But in a split second, we found ourselves safely out of the tunnel, and the big truck was past us, driving on down the hill on the other side. It was as if the concrete walls had temporarily expanded to let us pass. Neither vehicle had scraped the sides of the concrete tunnel or the other vehicle. Mirrors were still in place. What had just happened was physically impossible and totally illogical.

Silence prevailed in the station wagon. We were all speechless.

Finally, someone said, "What just happened?"

I said, "Did you just see that? Do you realize we just experienced a miracle?"

Someone said, "Good driving, Ms. Judy!"

Another person said, "It's like the truck was coming at us, then all of a sudden it was past us!"

"It's like we passed through each other somehow and came out the other side," another teen said, trying to wrap her head around what had transpired.

I can say with assurance that it was not because of my good driving. Not hitting the truck or the wall was unimaginable. I wasn't sure what happened or how, but I knew that God had intervened for that carload of children, the truck driver, and me. No matter which way it happened, it was a supernatural split second in time that should have ended in disaster.

As young people tend to do, when the shock wore off, they went back to laughing and talking about a number of things besides what we had just survived. Since none of them was driving, the full impact of the situation had perhaps escaped them.

I still drive that road on a regular basis. I never approach that tunnel without making sure no one is coming around the curve. Whenever I see a big truck coming, I hang back and make sure they have plenty of room to come through the tunnel. I'm always amazed at the size of a truck compared to the width of the tunnel, and then in my mind, I try to fit a station wagon in there with it. It's hard to say how many times I've tried to imagine that scenario again without disaster resulting.

I believe that on ordinary days, when we least expect it, there are supernatural interventions in people's lives all around us. Perhaps people don't recognize them as they go on their busy ways. Perhaps they don't acknowledge what they can't explain. I am persuaded that God extends His love and mercy to His children, as well as His supernatural protection.

In another outing, the group was much smaller. It was made up of four teens, another mother, and me. The other mom and I had decided to take the kids down to the Smoky Mountains and go tubing. It seemed like a fun thing to do on a Saturday. By that time seat belts were mandatory, and we never overcrowded a vehicle. As responsible adults, we were always aware of traffic safety, but none of us considered the risk that might be involved in tubing on the river.

Launching out into the water on our big black rental inner tubes seemed like the perfect idea for a sunny summer day. Somehow our little group got split up. I could see three of our group ahead in the water, but two were missing behind me. The three ahead were hanging onto low tree limbs at the edge of the river, waiting for the rest of us to catch up.

I turned my inner tube around in order to see if there was a problem and locate the missing two. Looking in that direction, I didn't see the huge log partially submerged behind me.

When my inner tube hit the tree, it flipped me off and facedown in the rushing water. The current literally shoved me under the log from my chest up. Desperately, I pushed against the loose gravel and silt on the river bottom. The water was too strong, and the loose pebbles were too unstable for me to push against and get any traction. Mud and stone slipped through my fingers as I struggled.

Sweet, cold water tried to push me forward. I was stuck, and I knew the people ahead of me could not get back in time to save me. The ones coming behind me were not going to be there fast enough.

The thought hit me: *You are going to die!*

In a fierce, rebellious response I cried out in my heart, *No! This is* not *my destiny. This is not how I'm going to die.*

A voice spoke calmly to me to stop fighting the current and the loose gravel and stick my hand straight up through the water as far as I could. I followed the directions, and a man's hand grasped mine.

I popped up out of the water like a fishing cork. There was no struggle, no pulling, no effort at all. I had been lodged under a tree, fighting for my life. Then suddenly, I was upright in the water and making my way to the shallower water closer to the riverbank.

My clothes were askew from the force of the current, and I was shaking all over. I looked at the man and said, "Had you not been here, I would have died. God sent you here to rescue me."

He smiled but said nothing. I lost track of him as the others managed to get to me from both directions. After I calmed down, we had miles to go down the river and back to our vehicles. I remained shaken the whole day, remembering the sensation of the cold water surging against me and my desperation as I clawed at the bottom of the river.

On the way home that night, I said to my son, "If the man on the log had not been there to pull me out, you would be driving to my funeral right now."

He had the most peculiar look on his face. "What man, Mom? What are you talking about?"

"The man who pulled me out from under the log!" I exclaimed.

"Are you talking about that little fat boy on the inner tube who floated past?" he asked.

"No! The man who pulled me out from under the log!"

"There was no man. What are you talking about? First you flipped off the inner tube and disappeared. We were trying to get back to you, and all of a sudden you just popped back up."

"What are *you* talking about? There was a man on the log who reached down and pulled me up!"

Needless to say, we were both perplexed. When we were reunited with the group, we rehearsed what had happened with them. The three ahead of me in the river had seen no man on the log or walking anywhere else. The two behind me had seen the man but didn't know where he had gone.

As for me, I believe exactly what I said to the man on the log in the middle of the river. "Had you not been here, I would have died. God sent you here to rescue me."

I often pray, "God, grant me the faith of a child to believe in the impossible and to recognize the heavenly supernatural working in our lives every day. Please don't let me get so full of logic, human intelligence, or doubt that I miss your intervention in my daily life. Help me to always believe in miracles."

A Room Full of Angels

Ronald C. Daniel

"If I'm going to die, I hope I will see an angel when the time comes."

As a hospice chaplain I had heard many requests from the terminally ill patients to whom I ministered, but this was the first time I had heard this one. This request came from Jill, one of my new home patients. She was forty years old, though she looked much younger, and had lost her hair due to the many treatments she had desperately tried as she valiantly fought her battle with cancer.

Jill was an attractive and intelligent woman who had overcome in her life what some would see as insurmountable obstacles. She and her sister had been abandoned by their mother when they were very young. Their father felt he couldn't take care of two small girls, so they were passed from one family member to another for several years. As soon as circumstances allowed, Jill stepped out into the world to try to make it on her own, but even then, life threw her some curve balls.

Along her difficult journey Jill had a son born with special needs. She realized she was not emotionally, physically, or financially able to care for his needs. As heart-wrenching as it was, she decided that the best opportunity for her son to receive the specialized care he would need was in a facility in California, where she was living at the time. Sometimes she had overwhelming feelings of guilt about what she had done, but she comforted herself in knowing that she had given him up out of love and wanting what was best for him. When I met Jill, she had not seen her son in many years.

Through sheer determination, Jill had worked her way through college and earned a degree in social work. She also met a man there named Jack, who would become her loving and devoted husband. Jack had a gentle spirit. As I watched him care for and support Jill, I couldn't help but think about how good God is to His children. In His infinite wisdom He knew exactly who and what Jill would need in the final months of her life.

In my conversations with her, I found that Jill had thought all of her bad times were behind her. She was married to a good man who loved her with a love like she had never experienced before. Even though it had taken many years, she had finally earned her degree and had begun a new career as a social worker. This had been the desire of her heart because she wanted to make a difference in the lives of hurting people. It seemed that all of her dreams had finally come to fruition.

But then tragedy struck. Jill was diagnosed with cervical cancer. She had believed in a higher power most of her life, having studied various spiritual beliefs and dabbled in different religions, but she had finally accepted the truth of a loving, sovereign God who sent His Son to die for her. She could not pinpoint the exact time this had happened, but she felt confident in her salvation. However, her faith was badly shaken when she was diagnosed with cancer. She began to question how a loving, compassionate God would allow this to happen just when she was experiencing the dream life.

Jill faced this challenge with the same tenacity as she'd faced all the other challenges in her life. She pursued every medical option available, including chemo and radiation, which often made her violently sick. At the same time, even though questions assailed her, she tried desperately to hold onto her faith. She vacillated between despair and believing that God would heal her.

But then the day came when the doctors told Jill they could do nothing else for her. Her cancer had continued to grow and spread, and it was time for her to make her final arrangements. At this time, hospice was called in to provide end-of-life comfort care, and I became her hospice chaplain. I was not aware that I was about to take an incredible journey with her.

During my first encounter with Jill at her home, I saw a young woman who was on an emotional roller coaster of despair one moment and euphoria the next. In a matter of minutes she could go from the mountaintop to the valley, from laughter to tears, from total denial to the reality of her impending death threatening to overwhelm her like a tsunami.

I quickly discerned that Jill's faith had been badly shaken, which was certainly understandable. As her chaplain, I tried to reinforce in her the truth that God's love for her had never faltered and never would. I couldn't give her an explanation for her illness because we will never receive the answers to some questions until we get to heaven, and then they will probably not seem as important as they do now. However, I encouraged her to hold on to God's promises of complete healing and inexpressible peace and joy that await us in heaven.

As I continued to visit Jill, and as her health continued to decline, I knew it was vital to help her reach a point of accepting God's will for her future, whatever it might be. When I first met Jill, she had asked if I believed in healing miracles, and I assured her that I did. I promised I would pray for that, but at the same time I began to introduce the truth that sometimes God does His healing work not in this life, but in the next. He would heal her in His way and on His terms.

Jill's journey was not all despair and tears. There were times of laughter as she shared good memories. More than once we talked about the possibility of Jill graduating, and this always brought a smile to her face. *Graduating* was our hospice term for a patient improving to the point that he or she no longer required our services. Jill loved to hear this and spoke of graduating and receiving a gold graduation certificate.

The weeks passed, and I began to see a shift in Jill's spirit. As I looked into her eyes, I saw that she understood that her journey was ending. She talked of healing and graduating less and asked more questions about what heaven is like. While she became more withdrawn as she grew weaker, I sensed a peace that I had not seen in her before.

I have often seen God's peace that passes all understanding settle upon His children as they approach their final hours, and that is beautiful to watch. Many struggle with doubt and fear, but as the end of life on earth approaches, God does a supernatural work of providing peace and comfort in their hearts and spirits. It was during this leg of her journey when Jill said, "If I'm going to die, I hope I will see an angel when the time comes."

Jill had asked us to promise that as she neared death, we would take her to our inpatient unit to die. We assured her that we would if we could. When I heard that she had been transported to the inpatient unit, I went to her room to see her.

By this time she was very weak, and talking was difficult for her, but when I entered the room, I knew something had changed. She was lying quietly in her bed with her eyes closed. When I called her name, she opened her eyes, smiled, and told me she was ready to graduate. I asked what she meant, and she said she was ready to graduate to heaven. She had finally found peace and acceptance. She was tired and ready to go.

I told her how happy I was for her and held her hand as I prayed for continued peace and comfort and a safe journey home. I assured her, as I often did with patients who were about to take that last part of their journey, that if I didn't see her again on this side, I would see her on the other side.

I did see Jill one more time before she stepped into eternity. When I entered her room this time, her husband, mother, and sister were present. Yes, her mother had come, and this was another challenge for Jill. She experienced a plethora of emotions concerning her mother's arrival, from anger about being abandoned as a child to a desire to know her mother loved her in spite of everything. Even though she never told me, I believe she had a peace about this, as well, by the time she reached the end of her remarkable journey on earth.

Jill's husband was sitting at her bedside, holding her hand. Jill looked like an angel—pale, eyes closed, but a beautiful picture of peace. Her husband said she had been talking all day about angels in the room. In fact, she kept saying there were too many angels crowding into the room.

I bent to whisper in her ear that I was there and it was time to let the angels escort her home. She smiled and whispered something again about angels. I knew this was the last time I would see Jill on this side of heaven, but I also knew she was ready to take the most amazing part of her journey.

That night Jill graduated to heaven, but that's not the end of the story. As related by those who were present, Jill went very peacefully with just a sigh and a smile on her face. And just as she took her last breath, there was a multitude of small bright flashes, like hundreds of lightning bugs in the room, and then they were gone. The angels had departed with Jill's spirit to a place of healing. God had granted her wish to see not only an angel, but a room full of angels.

Heaven does sometimes reach down to earth in ways that cannot be explained. These times are affirmations of God's love and the life He provides in the hereafter.

A Family in White Robes

Peggy Park

The hospital room was packed with visitors from the town some distance away where my patient lived. He was a new patient who could no longer talk due to his brain tumor. But he could still hear and respond with facial expressions and body language.

As I performed nursing duties, I realized I'd need to wait for another time to get to know his wife.

Upon entering the room on the second day I commented to his wife, Ellen, that the visitors were gone.

"They have all gone back home, and I don't know where to focus," she said sadly.

My heart went out to her. Not knowing anything about her religious beliefs, I took a chance and said, "I can tell you where to focus; let me go get my Bible."

"You can use mine," she said, and I knew I was talking to a woman who had some spiritual foundation. Her husband had a do-not-resuscitate order, so she was facing his impending death. Ellen was a schoolteacher and did not seem given to excessive emotions. She was calm and composed considering the circumstances.

I opened the Bible to Revelation 22:1–2 and read, "And he showed me a pure river of water of life, clear as crystal, proceeding from the throne of God and of the Lamb. In the middle of its street, and on either side of the river, was the tree of life" (NKJV).

I continued with Revelation 21:4, "And God will wipe away every tear from their eyes; there shall be no more death, nor sorrow, nor crying. There shall be no more pain, for the former things have passed away" (NKJV).

Ellen listened attentively, and her body seemed to relax. She became peaceful as the Scriptures seemed to soothe her.

Then I read my favorite verse about heaven, Revelation 4:3, which talks about the rainbow around the throne. That seemed to further comfort her.

After I read these verses I prayed for her aloud, being aware her husband might hear me. I prayed for comfort in the days to come, careful not to refer to his impending death. I prayed that God would strengthen her and be present with her in a way she could discern.

I was praying a very predictable prayer for the situation she faced.

Suddenly she said, "I saw it!"

"You saw what?" As she began to describe it, I said, "You had a vision?"

"Yes."

She had not known Jim's mother, yet she said his mother was in a white robe along with other family members waiting to welcome Jim. I was shocked as I had not anticipated her having a vision. Being a little skeptical, I asked again, "You had a vision?"

"Yes."

"Have you had visions before?"

"No."

The Lord had answered my prayer beyond anything I thought I was praying. I was absolutely amazed since I'd never learned anything about visions.

The next morning I went into the room, and Ellen exclaimed, "I saw it again this morning when I woke up. The family was there in white robes waiting to welcome Jim."

I was to be off duty for several days and asked her to write to me and let me know what happened if Jim passed while I was gone. Returning to work a few days later, I learned he was gone.

Eventually I found out more details when I received a letter from Ellen. Her sister-in-law had come near the end. Though the woman had never had a sense of smell, she reported smelling a sweet odor permeating the room, which I believe was the fragrance of Christ as described in 2 Corinthians 2:14–15. They saw a shadowy, angelic figure at the head of Jim's bed carry his spirit away.

I never saw Ellen again, but I rejoiced in her vision and the ministry of the Holy Spirit. It was wonderful to be a part of this answer to prayer where God did above anything I could ask or imagine.

A Heavenly Hand

E. V. Sparrow

The pine needles snapped and crunched beneath our feet on the red clay path through the oppressively hot woods—the only way that led to the swimming area of the Feather River near the town of Sloat and in the Sacramento Valley.

After doing our chores, we'd finally escaped from our stuffy four-room cabin in the logging camp. Our open, unscreened windows served as our air conditioner. Today, the air just hung like a wet blanket on a clothesline.

The scent of freshly cut pine from the mill blended with that of the smoked bacon that logging camp families cooked on their wood stoves. My tummy growled even though I'd had breakfast.

Did a twig snap a few feet away? Worry niggled through my thoughts.

Jill, my younger sister, trudged behind me. "Sis, wait up! Why are you in such a hurry?"

I glanced over the scene of tree trunks, shrubs, and large rocks. We often played hide-and-seek here.

We should've brought Gus. I always felt safer when our black lab came with us. If any pumas or bears came around, Gus would sound the alarm, but our brothers had taken him hunting.

A crow cawed above us, and goose bumps ran down my spine. "Too bad Dad had to work at the mill today. It would be more fun with him—even if he just fished." I glanced back again. *Just Jill.*

Jill stopped and looked around. "What's wrong?"

"Nothing. Just checking on you." I didn't want to spook her. "Remember Mom and Dad's river rules—stay near the sandbar, don't swim alone, don't go near the swift water, and watch out for drop-offs or holes in the riverbed."

We reached the rocky riverbank.

I listened. Then I scanned the forest and the path. *Nope. Nothing there.* "Mom said don't go past your knees." I dropped my towel on the bank. "You still have to learn how to swim." I grinned at Jill. "I learned at eight; you're ten."

Jill cringed. "I'm not going in! I don't like the water." She stuck her tongue out at me. "Just because you're fourteen doesn't mean you're so important." She put her hand on her hip. "Mom said even *you* can't go past the sandbar."

"I know that, silly." I rolled my eyes. "It's risky to go out far." I tossed my hair over my shoulder. "Even near summer's end."

Jill chose a shady spot under a crag, dropped on her towel, and grabbed her book.

At the water's edge, I squished my toes into the black, sandy river mud oozing between the granite boulders. Fool's gold sparkled and swirled to the surface before it floated away with the slow current. Standing half in and half out of the cold water made my legs ache. We kids learned it was best to get it over with. I plugged my nose and dunked under.

I swam out a few strokes away from the riverbank and searched for the sandbar. My feet bumped into the mound of sand. I seized a foothold. I watched the swift, white-capped water rush past me and heard its splashing. *Safe and calm here.*

A wave hit my torso. I squealed and twirled around. *What?*

One of the young kids from camp thrashed next to me. "Molly, go back—" Water splashed into my eyes and up my nose.

Molly screamed and fought for a foothold on the mound, but the water was too deep for her. She grabbed my arm and yanked me down so hard that the sandbar gave way under my feet.

I hauled us up to the surface and gulped in air mixed with some water. Dazed, I fought loose from Molly's grasp, coughed, and snatched a deep breath.

Jill's screams echoed around us.

Molly climbed onto my back and knocked me over. We slipped into the faster current of the dark-green water. Molly wrapped her legs over my shoulders, wound her arms around my head, and trapped me tight.

I opened my eyes, but I could only see murky water. My legs flailed in search of the sandbar, but Molly's weight anchored us. She clung to me and sank my hope for life. Minutes and our struggles intertwined until I couldn't move anymore. We descended deeper into the darkness.

The soft sound of bells, like wind chimes, swirled in the current around us. Peace poured into my mind and calmed my body. *It's not so awful to drown.*

In the depths below us, a golden light gleamed. It spread wider and drew near us.

My feet were about to touch it.

A hand pressed firmly against my back with Molly still coiled about me. The hand thrust us up to the surface and shoved us to the edge of the river. Water sprayed every which way as if we were on a motorboat. My hands and torso bumped into the steep riverbank.

The hand let go of me, and the water stilled.

Molly and I clawed through the mud and dragged ourselves out of the river. We rolled over and spewed out water like whales.

My chest heaved, and I gulped in lungfuls of sweet air.

Jill dropped to her knees in the mud and sobbed all over me.

"We're alive—" I wiped wet strings of hair off my face with the back of my muddy hand. My gasps slowed down, and I lay still, gathering my strength.

Smeared with muck, Molly slunk away. She didn't even say a word to us.

My heart slowed down. "Sis, who pushed us out of the water?" I leaned on my arm and scanned the area in search of our rescuer. "No one's here."

"No one came—I tried and tried to get help! I ran to that cabin, and no one was home—I screamed and screamed . . ." Jill wailed. "I thought you were going to die!"

"I'm all right, Sis."

"But you weren't all right! That brat Molly was climbing all over you! I kept screaming, 'Stop it!'" Jill shook and hyperventilated.

We clung to each other.

"It wasn't your fault . . . it's okay." I rocked Jill until she calmed down.

"Sis, we didn't break Mom and Dad's rules . . . but Molly snuck down here," she said. I shivered and shook like Jill.

"I couldn't save Molly." Memories spun in my thoughts like a record.

The sun finally thawed my frozen skin. "We can't always help. No matter how much we want to."

"Well, I wanted to!"

"It's okay. I know, Sis." I grabbed my towel, wrapped it around my shoulders, and grasped it with my fists. "I tried so hard . . . all my strength was used up fighting." My chin quivered on my knees, and I gulped down a sob. "I was too weak to save us."

Jill wiped her tears on my towel. "Who saved you?"

I shrugged. "It was too dark . . . until a golden light glowed underneath us." I stared at the river. "Then a hand pushed me and shoved us up and away . . . all the way back here. Next to you."

"Whose hand?"

"Don't know." *But I definitely felt a hand on my back.* I looked all around again. "You said no one came to help, right?"

Jill nodded, wide-eyed.

"Maybe . . . well, only God could help us . . . an angel?" I gazed at the slow dance of swirls flowing with the river's eddy. "Perhaps an angel beneath the Feather River."

The Little Girl in the White Dress

CARYL HARVEY

She was tiny, frail, and as white as the sheets that encased her. The only signs that the little girl was awake were the faint moans that came from her mouth. They weakly escaped with a dry, crackling noise that alarmed her young mother. Shawna rose from the chair beside the hospital bed and searched her four-year-old daughter's face for signs of change. The fuzzy stuffed rabbit, unnoticed at the child's side, seemed forlorn; Shawna picked it up, pulled it close to her face, and rocked it.

On rounds, the doctor had checked Brittany's pulse, put his hand on her clammy forehead, and listened to her heartbeat. He had shrugged.

"Well, no news is good news."

Earlier, when he had admitted his little patient, his eyes were red and his voice shook. "If she makes it through the next eight hours . . ." he had said, his voice trailing off.

Shawna nodded. She had prayed until she was sick of praying. She and her daughter had struggled against this enemy, this leukemia, for a year. Both of them were tired. She didn't want to admit it, but maybe they were defeated, too. Maybe God had other things on His mind than a sick little girl with blond curls and blue eyes.

When Brittany was first diagnosed at three, her doctor cried. He said he knew little about acute lymphocytic leukemia. Her best chance was to go to Children's Hospital in Denver, 176 miles away. He prayed with her family and hurried them on their way.

When they arrived at the hospital, Brittany was a ball of energy. She ran and giggled, climbing on the jungle gym with other children in the waiting area. She looked as healthy as any child. Two hours later, lying in a crib with an IV sending lifesaving but poisonous chemotherapy coursing through her veins, she was the sickest child Shawna had ever seen. The little girl crawled to the farthest corner of the crib when doctors or nurses entered the room. She chattered in baby talk and forgot her toilet training. Shawna sat beside her while she was awake, and she slept in the plastic-upholstered recliner in the room at night. Every two or three hours, the nurses entered to check on the child, and Shawna woke to listen to their whispers, hoping to catch a few words about Brittany's condition.

The year that followed was a nightmare. Brittany endured two surgeries to place ports in her chest so that they could administer the treatment more easily. She faced hundreds of pricks and pokes with sharp needles, and hours of nausea. The preschooler lost her hair and gained weight as a result of taking prednisone. She wore a backpack that held a container of the chemo drug and infused it constantly into her little body. Shawna learned how to clean the port. She became an expert at changing out the needles and tapes so that the nurses in the small-town hospital just stepped back when Brittany had appointments and let her mother work.

Shawna prayed, too. She prayed for healing and for strength. She asked for assurance and then consolation. Finally, she just became silent before God and let Him read her heart. She was so tired. God seemed far away and deathly still. Somehow she had to face the truth: Her child might not survive.

The months dragged on, and Brittany's care became routine. On days when her white blood cell count was low, visits were discouraged. On good days, people were welcome, but they had to wash their hands before they settled into a visit, and they couldn't see Brittany if they were sniffling or felt ill. Brittany had reverted to wearing diapers, and they had to be disposed of in hazardous waste containers. Once, at the county fair, her port came out, and Shawna and Brittany rushed to the emergency room so Brittany could be treated for chemical burns.

Slowly, Brittany got stronger. She accepted having to stay awake until the visiting nurse came to change her medications at ten in the evening. She got used to the frequent trips to the hospital in Denver for checkups. She abandoned the baby talk to which she had reverted during her first stay at Children's Hospital and sounded more like the four-year-old she was. There was a new normal in the family, and everyone embraced it; they were soldiers battling for Brittany's life.

She started preschool. Shawna held her breath. Children could be so cruel, and Brittany was chunky and bald. Brittany's grandfather declared he would shave his own head if the children made fun of his granddaughter. He needn't have worried. Brittany was the only child in class who could clap her head and hand together to the nursery songs they sang. Her classmates were enthralled. But the many victories preceded setbacks, and Brittany's climb to "better" was exhausting for her and for her mother.

They probably should not have taken her on the family vacation, but she had seemed so much stronger. Brittany enjoyed Branson, Missouri, although she tired easily. She fell asleep aboard the paddle wheel boat cruise, leaving her meal untouched. Later that night she spiked a high fever, and her parents and grandfather rushed her to the Branson hospital. Unaccustomed to treating critically ill children, the doctors sent the little girl to the Springfield hospital. She woke the next morning and asked her mother, "Is my vacation over?"

It was over. The hospital released Brittany on the condition that the family take her home, all the way to northeast Colorado, and get her into a hospital. They stopped in Carthage, Missouri, so the little girl, her sisters, and cousins could see the Precious Moments Chapel. Brittany's grandfather wheeled her through the buildings in a stroller, and she slept. He bought her a doll and placed it in her arms. She didn't respond.

God wasn't responding, either. He didn't show up on the trip. No one heard His voice in the emergency room when they rushed Brittany to the hospital. There were no thundering words of assurance or whispered words of peace from heaven. Shawna was alone with her child in the room, and the only sounds were muffled footsteps, voices in the hall, and the chirps of the machinery monitoring Brittany's vital signs.

So they waited. Eight hours felt interminable, and yet it was like a moment. Shawna was weary of the battle, but these hours could easily be the last she would spend with her daughter. Her mom had always believed in prayer, hadn't she? That is, she had until her son, Shawna's brother, Chad, was murdered. It took a year for her to pray again.

How long would it take Shawna to forgive God if He took her baby? Maybe the whole thing was a joke and there was no God. She shrank back from that thought; she knew He existed. At this point, though, she doubted He cared.

There was nothing else to do. The young mother prayed again and waited.

This time, though, things were different. Brittany looked different. Better. The doctor confirmed it when he came to check on her. The fever was down, and she was resting. She had color, and it was pink, not yellow. She had made it through the critical eight hours and beyond. When the medical staff entered the room to perform their duties, they were no longer somber. They even joked and laughed. Everyone seemed overcome with relief at the change in Brittany's condition, and that told Shawna that the battle had been won.

Later, as the young mother sat beside the crib reading to her girl, Brittany sat up in bed.

"Mommy," she asked, "who was that little girl who stood by my bed all night?"

Shawna gasped. God certainly wouldn't desert them again and let Brittany lapse into delirium. "What little girl, honey?"

"The little girl in the white dress. She smiled at me, and I thought you saw her, too. She was nice."

Shawna quizzed Brittany. Surely her daughter had dreamed the visitor who stood guard through the night. Brittany remained adamant that a little girl had been there. She had made her feel safe and helped her rest. Brittany repeated the story to her father, to the doctors and nurses, and finally, to her pastor, who had no doubt about the mystical girl's identity.

Faith is believing in something you can't see. Adults come to accept that and often miss the angels that God sends to minister to His people. Children see the world through faith, and their faith allows them to see miracles. They understand that the divine is around us all the time, in rainbows of promise, in provision and peace, and in a little girl's guardian angel who stood watch until death gave up and left the building.

An Angel on Her Bed

Dee Aspin

Liz was the expressive one from the beginning. She was as free as the Frisbee she flung in our high school quad at lunch, and her infectious laugh rose above the chatter. Amused, I'd glance up from my brown-bag lunch as I sat with miniskirted gossips in our clique. Holes in her faded polo shirt and baggy shorts didn't bother Liz whenever she ran up to say hello, toss her golden-streaked hair, joke, and run off.

I think God knew Liz was one of His kids who would need an angel working overtime, and I was the friend who would need a companion for an auspicious occasion—Mom's eightieth birthday.

Although opposites, Liz and I forged a deep friendship through our faith in Jesus. We were both from broken homes, we shared a common love for nature, and we attended the same nursing program. Mom dubbed her a second daughter.

Now, she sat in the driver's seat, tapping the wheel. The San Francisco hotel rooms were booked and restaurant reservations made—per Mom's birthday wishes. Everyone had left . . . except us.

"We need to go!" Liz backed the car out from the driveway and ignored my protests from the passenger's seat. "We'll be late meeting everyone if we keep waiting for your mom's friend. It's her problem—not ours."

I fought guilt but settled back for our ride. Liz merged onto Interstate 80 and breezed into easy conversation, becoming more reflective as we neared the City by the Bay. For years our friendship had vacillated between excellence and emptiness. Only recently, in the past two years, had our friendship renewed. It felt like old times for us to be on the road again.

"I was born in San Francisco's Panhandle district, Sis. I went to Catholic school and traded peanut butter sandwiches for Asian rice balls with the Japanese students. I learned to surf in the bay . . ."

Liz described the years she and her twin, John, watched their mom orbit in and out of mental institutions for electric shock therapy—the treatment of choice for schizophrenia during the '60s. Her dad orbited, too, loaded with liquor, half-present—better gone. Her Spanish-speaking grandparents across the street helped raise her and John.

Liz and John's one wish was to take care of their mom when they turned eighteen. But at thirteen they watched as their mom was whisked away in an ambulance for the last time—she died at the hospital. They were transported by police cars to the San Francisco juvenile hall as wards of the state.

My angst had long passed, and Liz's voice strained over the road noise.

"That was the worst night of my life, Sissy. I was terrified. They separated John and me and locked me in a cell. I hugged my knees and cried out to God. It took four months to get released to my aunt's care. Dad tied everyone up with legal red tape because he didn't want anyone else to take care of us. My aunt already had my older brother, Matt, and we wanted to live with her, too."

The traffic slowed in Fairfield. Liz scowled. "I hate my dad, Sis. I don't know if he's dead or alive, and I don't care. I never want to see him again after what he did to John."

A lone sea gull soared over our car as sadness swelled within me and Liz relived her loss.

"I told John not to let Dad back into our lives, but John was too nice. I didn't even know Dad was in town until John called me at work crying, 'I can't take it anymore—Dad's trashed my place.'

"I was furious! 'Why did you let the devil in your apartment?' I asked. I left work and chased Dad out of John's place and told him never to come back to Sacramento. John had his first schizophrenic episode soon after and committed suicide two years later."

Memories of that terrible time jarred my thoughts.

Then, Liz's voice softened. "One morning, after Phil and I married, he stood by a chest of drawers, and I thought he was John. I remembered what you said after John died, when you drove from the Bay Area to see me."

I glanced at Liz. "You mean when I said God would provide a husband someday who would be a comfort to you, as John had been?"

"Yes." Her turquoise eyes sparkled.

How could Liz remember? She had lain curled up on her side and rocked on her bed for three weeks after John's death. Her aunt said she'd occasionally let my brother, Michael, hold her. I had felt helpless standing there as she moaned in mental darkness.

During the three-hour drive to visit her, I had sung worship songs we both loved. I told Liz I loved her and prayed for her—and that I felt God had given me a message for her. Then, I had doubted it would make any difference in her shocked state and wondered if I was just trying to comfort her with my own hope.

Liz flipped a blond curl out of her eye. "You know, Sis, I love my Pooh Bear, Phil, and my Pooh Bear loves me. He works so hard—sometimes I worry about him. He seems tired a lot lately. If something happens to Phil, I'll never marry again. We have three wonderful boys—I love my boys." I nodded. A flock of swallows looped in the distant sky.

"You know, Sis, I just can't believe God sent me an angel when I got kicked out of nursing school."

"Really, Liz? I'd forgotten all about it."

"I think about it all the time. That God loved me so much, He sent me an angel. It's all my fault. I wasn't studying like I should have. I was running around, and my study habits were bad . . ."

Running around. Hardly. Liz worked full-time, even in nursing school, and sunk most of her spare time, then and later, into helping humanity—buoying the spirits of anyone who had a grief, loss, or sickness.

"I thought I could just get by until one day when Mrs. George, the medical-surgical instructor, called me into her office and said, 'Liz, you failed the test. You're out of the program.'

"I couldn't believe my ears. I begged, 'No, please Mrs. George—give me another chance.'

"Mrs. George was firm. 'No, Liz, I'm sorry. You're amazing in clinical—you're the best. But you don't have the discipline to study, and it takes both.'

"I gathered my books, drove home sobbing, then fell on my bedroom floor and cried out, 'I don't know what to do, God. What will I do with my life if I can't be a nurse?' I was engulfed in despair. I didn't know how much time had passed when suddenly, I sensed something in the room and looked up.

"I couldn't believe my eyes. An angel was sitting on my bed. He was huge. Bright and white and beautiful. His head was all the way up to the ceiling. I got up and sat at the foot of the bed next to him. I just sat there staring at him. I didn't feel fear. He was the most beautiful thing I'd ever seen. And the peace . . . I felt total peace. Nothing mattered anymore. I couldn't believe it. God sent me an angel!"

When I turned to catch a glimpse of her face, Liz looked radiant.

"I was so happy just to be with *my* angel. I don't know how much time went by." Liz gazed at the East Bay and palmed the wind from her open window. "Then, around midnight the phone rang suddenly. It was Mrs. George. I was surprised she was calling me so late. She offered me a chance to take the test again."

Liz laughed. "I got off the phone and called Lily, the brain of the class, and asked if I could borrow her notes. She offered to help. We studied together all night—I took the test the next morning and passed."

The traffic slowed in the East Bay. We inhaled sea air. Liz lightly tapped my shoulder, and I looked at her. She broke into her classic grin, and I smiled back.

"Sis, who would've thought I'd go on to get my master's at Sonoma State and meet my husband?" Bay Bridge cables appeared in the distance.

"And that we'd have three beautiful boys—they're seventeen, fifteen, and now, Sammy? Can you believe he just turned thirteen?" Liz gushed with motherly pride.

"They're good boys, Sis. They love Jesus. They all help out in the community. It means so much to me—I've really drilled it into them that they are brothers, and family always need to be there for each other. And I really feel they will do well in life . . . that they will all do just great! God has blessed me more than I could have ever imagined. And I still can't believe God sent me an angel. It was the most beautiful thing, Sis. The most beautiful thing."

"It really is amazing, Liz," I marveled. "Who would have known when we were young what God would do?"

The familiar skyscrapers silhouetted against the pale-blue sky lifted my spirit as the Golden Gate Bridge sparkled in the distance. We felt as peaceful as the whitecaps lilting on the sea.

Liz continued to reminisce, up to the present joy of celebrating Mom's eightieth together in the city where she and my dad were born. It felt like a circle of life. We were in a significant place and experiencing a life-defining moment.

Later that evening, Liz received a phone call. Her middle son had broken his arm playing baseball. She left immediately, saying, "I want to set it." She called us when she arrived home at one in the morning to tell us that all was well.

I never saw Liz again. Two weeks later, she died from a septic pneumonia contracted where she worked as an ER nurse practitioner. Flags were lowered to half-mast in front of the medical center, and the funeral home bulged with over five hundred people, including the staff who loved her. The following day a friend and I wept en route to console her family at their rural country home.

Looking back, I was humbled to realize God gave us the gift of friendship and a special time to reminisce alone one last time.

Liz's precious words, expressions of her heart, and hopes for her husband and sons had been entrusted to me during that serendipitous drive. I felt profound purpose and compassion from God as I shared them with her husband . . . a precious cargo of words to help ease the pain of his loss.

We were all comforted knowing Liz was safe with her Lord Jesus, her twin, John, and her guardian angel.

Liz's oldest son has since married, and he named his firstborn Elizabeth. The circle continues.

Second Breath

Elfriede Volk

He said he couldn't handle life with her anymore. Exasperated, our son-in-law explained that she wasn't the same person, and he wanted to put her in an institution.

He was talking about his wife, Karen, our daughter. Working two jobs to pay debts her husband had accrued, she was rushing to her second job when she had a bicycle accident and suffered a head injury. In the two years since then, instead of getting better, she had gotten worse.

"Can she fly?" my husband asked.

"I think so."

"Then fly her home. I'll wire you the money for the ticket. Just let us know when to expect her so we can be waiting at the airport."

He hung up the phone and looked at me. "You okay with that?"

"Of course. I just wish I knew more of what to expect and how to deal with her injury and mood swings."

We picked Karen up at the Kelowna airport the next afternoon. She seemed dazed, spaced-out. Having crossed three time zones, she was also exhausted. We had no chance to talk. She went to bed right after supper.

"I will need to go to the church school first thing in the morning," I told my husband as he helped me with the dishes. "The cherries are ripe, and we have several orders to fill. At our last meeting, the board decided to let some of the kids help with the picking, but I'm not comfortable with that."

Besides the school building and playing field, the school property had a small cherry orchard. Sales of the cherries helped with expenses. The trees were tall, and the ground was rather steep. Ideal for sledding in the winter, but hazardous for novices working with ladders. As chairman of the board, I felt it my duty to do most of the picking. After all, I had fifty years of experience working in and operating an orchard, so I was aware of the dangers. Planning to start picking as soon as the sun rose the next day, I turned in early, too.

I woke to a darkness deeper than night. Somewhere a bird called loudly, incessantly, irritatingly. I wanted it to stop so I could go back to sleep, but it wouldn't. I tried to identify it, but I had never heard that kind of call before. High-pitched, wheezing, almost gurgling. Then I heard another call.

"Mrs. Volk. Mrs. Volk, are you all right?" a young girl's voice asked.

"Yes, of course I am," I answered, annoyed to think that a stranger had come into my bedroom. I tried to sit up to see who it was, but my head felt too heavy. It wouldn't move. Neither would my eyelids. When they finally opened, the blackness turned to green. Leafy, swaying, scintillating green. My lids fell shut again.

The bird was still calling, louder, drowning out the ringing in my ears. My head was pounding and felt as if it would explode. Forcing my eyes open, I tried to see where the bird was and where I was. Unable to lift my head, I rolled over to push myself up. My hands felt something cool and grassy. Looking down, I saw that I *was* lying on grass with my head hanging over a retaining wall. Pulling my legs underneath me, I pushed myself up into a sitting position. As I did so, the bird sound grew fainter, and the gurgling stopped. Then, as my eyes began to focus, I saw red cherries among the green leaves.

I also saw a twelve-foot ladder lying beside me, its foot-end jutting out over the retaining wall adjacent to the orchard.

I tried to get up, but my legs wouldn't support me. Though even the slightest movement took great effort, I knew I couldn't remain sitting there. On my hands and knees, I slowly crawled to the base of the nearest cherry tree and leaned against its trunk, closing my eyes and panting from the exertion. When I opened my eyes again, I saw a picnic table just beyond the tree, so I crawled there. I pulled myself onto the bench so that I could sit and see and think. That's where my husband found me.

"What happened to you?" he asked. "You look terrible! Did you fall?"

I ignored his questions. "Who's that with you?" I asked.

He stared at me, concern etching his face. "You don't even recognize your own daughter?" he exclaimed. "That's Karen."

"Karen? Why? What's she doing here? When did she come?"

He looked at me, then at Karen, then me again. "We'd better get Mom to the hospital," he said, motioning to Karen. "I think she fell and hit her head."

Karen came to my other side. Together they helped me up and supported me as I staggered to the car.

Lying on a gurney in the emergency ward, I was hooked up to a monitor that kept beeping as my blood pressure kept dropping. Not wanting to alarm me, someone shut it off. Then the doctor came in. He examined me, feeling for fractures. I gritted my teeth so that I would not scream.

"Do you know what day it is?" he asked.

I looked at him blankly.

"I'll give you a hint," he said. "It's a very important day for Canada."

I was stumped.

"It isn't Canada Day," he prompted.

"An election?" I finally ventured.

"Bingo!" he said. "You can go home."

"Go home?" my husband asked. "What about X-rays?"

"Unfortunately, the X-ray department is extremely busy right now," the doctor said. "Her arms and legs aren't broken, and as far as her ribs are concerned, these types of fractures don't always show up on X-rays. And even if they do, there isn't much one can do about them anyway."

But I could feel them and hear them when I moved, and the ends of the broken ribs grated against each other. People could even see them, and a lump underneath my left breast grew to grapefruit size.

"A collection of blood and calcium that leached out of your ribs," our family doctor said. "It will eventually be reabsorbed by your body."

What I had assumed to be bird calls had been my punctured lungs struggling to take in air. With damaged lungs, even talking took great effort. After only a few words, I ran out of breath and had to pant to get more air. Whatever I did was done in slow motion, deliberately, painstakingly, carefully.

Some of my injuries were obvious, but there were others not as visible, but nonetheless distressing. There was partial amnesia. I could not remember picking Karen up at the airport the day before. Some things were completely erased from my memory. I had to concentrate to remember how to turn on the stove, to make sense of the seemingly jumbled words and letters on a page, to follow a recipe.

When I closed a door, I had to remind myself that it was the doorknob that was turning, and not the house, despite what I seemed to see. Stationary things appeared to be moving, while moving things appeared to be stationary.

Unable to do much physically, I had time to think. And I thought a lot, going over the events leading up to my fall, over and over again. As usual, after setting up the ladder, I had tested it, standing on the bottom rung, grasping both sides firmly, and swaying back and forth to make sure it would not slip. Yet it did. And as my ladder slipped, I was catapulted headfirst down to the retaining wall and toward the concrete pad below. But I didn't fall on the concrete pad. My hip broke my fall by hitting the edge of one of the rungs, breaking it in the process. The resultant bruise stretched from my waist to halfway down my thigh.

My left arm also broke my fall, hitting the double boards at the base of the ladder and cushioning my rib cage, preventing more serious injury. I shuddered as I remembered that ten years earlier my brother, while a passenger in a friend's car, had been in a collision. His seat belt had broken a rib, which punctured his heart, and he had died instantly. That could have happened to me, too, I realized.

"Why?" I asked. Why did God keep me from going over the wall and cracking my head open? Why did He allow the rib to puncture my lung but not my heart? Why did He spare me?

A few weeks before my accident, a friend who operated a greenhouse had been standing on a six-foot ladder, hanging ornamental flower baskets on lampposts. His ladder slipped, and he fell. He was killed instantly. I was on top of a twelve-foot ladder, with a six-foot drop-off behind me. I was catapulted backward, yet I didn't die. Why?

Two weeks after my fall, a friend's husband was helping a neighbor trim some branches from a tree. One branch swung back, knocking him down and breaking his back. After spending a year in the hospital and rehab, he still died. Why? Why him and not me?

Some people who have had near-death experiences claim they saw a bright light. I didn't. I saw only darkness—deep, black, ultimate darkness. But through it all, I also saw God. Not physically, for no mortal can see Him, but I saw His great love for me and all mankind. Not just in sparing my life, but also in giving me understanding and greater compassion.

When I was in high school, friends called me Madam Einstein because learning came easily and I always got 100 percent on my tests. After my fall and concussion, I realized that for some people learning is a struggle, that they may not see things the same way I do, that they may be battling handicaps others are unaware of, that they may have difficulty remembering things. And having now experienced these problems myself, I have more patience and compassion for them.

Having suffered a debilitating concussion, I could also relate better to my daughter and understand what she was going through. At first, she became my caregiver. Then, when her husband emailed her saying he wanted a divorce, I looked after her. I was there to comfort her, support her, sit with her, and hold her through the long nights when she didn't want to live anymore. In that way, my injuries became a blessing.

Some people see God in the light, when everything is going well, but I found that in the darkness His mercy and grace shone through the brightest.

The Bible tells us that God created mankind in His own image. I believe that involves not only physical appearance, but also character. Into this inanimate form, God breathed the breath of life, and Adam became a living soul.

When I fell in that cherry orchard I could have, and probably should have, died. But God, in His mercy, gave me a second chance. He restored to me the breath of life, and I now want to live wholly for Him.

Room with a View

MIDGE DESART

I was driving aimlessly around the waterfront in my city, so tired I felt the weight bearing down on my shoulders, but I couldn't go home.

My husband of fifty-four years was struggling with Parkinson's disease and cancer, and as his caregiver I was struggling with him.

We both had sleepless nights as the demons of dementia haunted his sleep, and mine, as he demanded to know why I let the monsters that I couldn't see ruin our home. He was sure they were preparing to evict us.

A loving caregiver friend, Clarene, gave several hours a week so I could grocery shop and run necessary errands. I had finished my to-do list for the day, but I resisted going home because I didn't have the energy to cope with the pressure of being on call all day and all night. I was at the end of my tether. My conversation with God went like this: *I'm so tired. Help.*

I stopped the car at a park near our home. Sitting quietly and looking at the beautiful Puget Sound and the majestic Olympic Mountains across the wide expanse of water calmed my heart.

An idea popped into my head. What if I found a small space to rent where I could write and spend quiet time while a caregiver was taking care of my husband?

My conversation with God continued: *Dear heavenly Father, I know it's selfish, but it would be nice to have a retreat. I'd be happy with an office space where I could have my coffeepot, a restroom, maybe a little fridge for snacks, a table for my computer, and of course an Internet connection. If I don't find anything, I'll know it's not your will. Amen.*

For three weeks, I used every moment away from home to search for office rental space or a very small apartment. I looked online and kept running into dead ends.

I contacted a real estate agent, Shane. By this time my list included a view of the water as a must-have. After all, if a few minutes of relaxing by the water calmed my soul, I could only imagine the benefits I'd reap from hours of reflecting on God's creation.

I drove by several apartments for rent with a water view. I pictured myself moving in with a short list of belongings.

I found an old house with a studio apartment for rent on the top floor. A flight of steep wooden stairs led up the outside of the home to the apartment. I was willing to overlook the fact that it rains every other day, which would make the stairs slippery. If I carried anything that weighed more than three ounces it would be a challenge, and did I dare consider computer gear?

I was sure this was my dream place as I proceeded to ignore all the red flags. After all, it checked off three boxes on my list: water view, small studio, and a good price—did

I mention water view? Not considering the mega flight of stairs an issue, in my mind, I was already moving in. I almost cried when I found out it was rented—as was everything else on my drive-by-and-look list.

By this time my dream place was evolving. Now I wanted a small house, a beach cottage, with a water view. Shane made a valiant attempt to help until a sad day when I received his text saying no such place existed in the parameters I'd outlined.

Two vacation homes were available on an island in the Sound—with ferry access twice a day. If you didn't get off the island by six you were staying overnight—not a good fit for people with medical issues. I crossed them off the list quickly.

It was discouraging, but I was sticking by my original prayer that if it wasn't His will, I wouldn't find a place.

The next day I needed to mail a letter. Though my dream cottage didn't exist, that wouldn't stop me from enjoying the view that was less than a mile from my home. I decided if I couldn't have a cottage overlooking the water, I would use my free time to drive to the nearest post office, which was eight minutes from our house in the tiny town of Steilacoom, Washington.

Mailing a letter was only one of my errands. I also needed groceries, and I only had about three hours to get everything done.

I dropped my mail in the box and started back the way I'd come, heading for the grocery store. Two blocks from the post office on the same block as the studio apartment with the steep stairs was a little sign on the sidewalk: For Rent. I glanced at the sign as I drove by and thought, *What's for rent? All the houses in this area are mansions. I should know; I've checked everything.*

I kept driving, but something compelled me to turn around and get the phone number. I wrote down the number and continued up the small street to turn around and head for the grocery store. At the top of the street on a little knoll all its own was an old, tiny house overlooking the water—exactly what I had in my mind. It had a For Rent sign in the window with the same phone number. I drove into the driveway and dialed the number. In my heart I told myself, *There is no way this place isn't already rented.*

A man's voice said, "Leave a number, and I'll call you back."

It was the voice of doom, as I was positive he wouldn't call back.

I prayed, *Dear Lord, if this place isn't mine please help me to have a good attitude. I know you didn't promise something frivolous like this. You've blessed us beyond what we need, and I'm thankful for what we have. Even though it would be just what I had in mind.*

Before I backed out of the driveway, my phone rang. It was the owner. He said, "Are you interested in the house?"

"Am I? It's just what I've been searching for. Is it rented?"

He said, "No, I just put the sign up."

I said, "I want it."

"Would you like me to send you a rental agreement? Or if you like, come back to the house at one thirty and I'll show you around."

"I'll be there at one thirty." I was so excited my stomach was doing flip-flops.

I prayed, *God, I feel like you led me to this little old house in the middle of mansions. I can handle the rental price, but if it's not going to be mine, help me to accept that without question.*

It was twelve thirty, and I still had to grocery shop. I drove to the store with shaking hands. I had to be at the tiny house when the owner got there. I was so afraid someone else would grab it.

It was my quickest shopping trip ever. I grabbed everything on my list as if I were being timed. I searched for the smallest line; of course, it's never the one you're in. After checking out, I ran for the door and was back at the tiny house with thirty minutes to spare.

My heart dropped to my stomach when I saw a car parked in the drive. Once again that doomed feeling took control. You might say at this point, "O ye of little faith," and you would be correct. But I didn't know if my selfish wish was worthy of God's attention. I didn't want to be one of those people, which I clearly was, who expected God to grant all their wishes like a good fairy.

I walked up and nodded to the driver. "Are you the owner?" I asked.

He said, "No, I'm waiting for him."

Oh no. I was sure he was waiting to look at the house.

I walked around the house to the patio and paced while looking at the most stunning view in the neighborhood—the water with the Olympic Mountains on the other side and ferries scuttling back and forth to the islands. There was a view of the Narrows Bridge in the distance.

And then there were three. Another man parked on the street and approached the house. He looked at the sign in the window and wrote the phone number down. Then he came back to the patio. "Are you the owner?" he asked.

I shook my head and said, "I'm waiting for the owner."

He said, "Do you want to rent this house?"

"Yes, I really want it," I said. Think of a three-year-old who wants candy. I'm sure that's what I sounded like. I was afraid this man was going to take my tiny house away from me.

He laughed. "Okay, I won't hassle you, but I'll keep the number in case you change your mind." He drove away, and I sighed with relief, but there was still the guy in the driveway.

Another car came, and a man got out to talk to the man parked in the driveway. The two men shook hands and came around to the patio.

I felt deflated—doomed to failure. They'd already shaken hands on a deal. How could I feel so possessive over something I didn't have? I reminded myself of the blessings God had given us and the needs He had met in our lives.

The owner put his hand out. "Hello, I'm Brad. We spoke on the phone."

I smiled the way you do at church when people ask, "How are you?" and you feel lousy. My eyes strayed to the other man.

Brad said, "This is my contractor. He's doing the renovation of the house, refinishing the hardwood floors, and painting."

My smile grew much bigger. "I was afraid he was a renter." I was breathless.

"No, you're the first one to see the house," Brad said.

I didn't need to see the house. I wanted it, but I followed him in. All I could say was, "It's perfect; just what I was looking for. I want it. Can I put a deposit down?"

Brad said, "If you want to, but don't you want to see the rental agreement? I can send it to you, and after you've looked it over, we'll go from there."

"I'm afraid to wait. I know you won't understand, but I've been looking for this house, and in case you didn't know, there are no rentals in this whole town. It's a miracle that I found this when I did."

"Just so you understand, we're still renovating. It will be a few weeks before we're finished."

"That's okay. It doesn't matter. I should explain I'm looking for a retreat. I'm a writer, painter, quilter, and beading embellishment artist. This will be a perfect environment for all of those things, and I'll take really good care of it."

I wrote a deposit check on the spot and drove home very excited. I was thanking God for leading me to the perfect retreat—and asking myself, *What just happened?*

When I got home I told Clarene that God had given me the little house of my dreams. She rejoiced with me. She was the one person who truly understood my need to have a sanctuary.

Telling my children and my husband was a little more intimidating. I faced questions like "What were you thinking?" followed by "Can we stay there sometime?"

My daughter, granddaughters, friends, and I have had some special times together in the cottage. My son and his wife want to spend a weekend there, and the whole family is looking forward to the Fourth of July when the town sets off the firework display out on the water in front of my tiny house.

God doesn't promise life will be perfect. My husband is still ill, and I have my aches and pains, but God's love is evident in our lives as He blesses us in little and big ways that say, "I know you're hurting, but that doesn't mean I don't love you."

Unexplained blessings are God's way of letting us know He's with us in the good times and the bad—always.

Jesus said, "Lo, I am with you always, even unto the end of the world" (Matthew 28:20 KJV).

Think of it: a tiny house, eight minutes from my home, with a view of the water, in a town that has no available rentals. Anything that goes on the market is snapped up in minutes.

I can only believe one thing: God cares for me. He knows what I need.

There are so many words from God that come to mind, but one verse stands out: "Every good gift and every perfect gift is from above, and cometh down from the Father of lights" (James 1:17 KJV).

A funny thing happened on the way to the post office. Without warning God smiled at me and gave me the desire of my heart.

When God Flexed His Muscles

Craig Nelson,
as told to Ronica Stromberg

There are only two things you need to know about me—two important things that have happened in my nearly sixty years.

The first is that I was saved when I was four years old in Ottertail, Minnesota, in a Missouri Synod Lutheran church. I went through the rest of my childhood knowing and loving God.

The second happened in 1977, when I was seventeen years old, playing high school football in Nebraska. I was a senior at Wakefield High School and hadn't put a lot of thought into what might happen after high school. My parents were farmers who saw hard work as the way to get ahead. College was deemed unnecessary. So I followed my father's lead in life, working hard on the farm and taking vocational trade courses at school. I didn't have much time for fun, but when I did, I knew what I wanted to do: play football.

I played my first three years of high school, never garnering much attention, but that year, my senior year, I stood six feet four, weighed 215 pounds, and ran fast. I played offensive tackle and defensive end nearly the whole game, every game. Coach had noticed me.

I was halfway through the season when I realized my playing days were almost over, and consequently, my team's remaining games became even more important to me. In the next game, on a Friday, another player tackled me hard, tearing into my right leg and leaving me with a painfully deep thigh bruise.

I had been hurt before and expected the injury to get better over the weekend. It didn't. At practice on Monday, I could barely force myself down into a football stance, and when I did, an all-consuming pain stabbed through the muscles of my right leg and radiated to the rest of my body.

Coach saw I was hobbled by pain and told me to go into the locker room early. I did, and he joined me shortly.

"Craig," he said, "our next game is really important. We need you. You're going to have to tough it out. Do whatever you must do to get ready to play."

I agreed with him, but I didn't know how I would play the game when even sitting and standing hurt. Since my parents were farmers, we didn't run to the doctor or get medicine for every little thing. I figured Coach was right: I was going to have to tough it out somehow.

That night, after eating dinner, I went straight to my room and lay down. The room was still, quiet, and dark. I began praying to God about my pain and anxiety.

"God, you need to help me," I prayed. "I can't do this without you."

His words "Be still, and know that I am God" (Psalm 46:10) came to me and blanketed me. I continued praying and meditating for hours until I finally fell asleep.

That next day, Tuesday, my team had an away game, and we met to practice before it. My leg felt as if it were getting stabbed every time I moved it. Too soon, the game started. From the beginning and throughout it, I launched prayer after prayer to God, asking Him to help me withstand the pain and play well. The prayer seemed to work like armor. Enough of the pain was blocked out that I was able to play very well, and we won.

My relief was short-lived because we had another game three days later, and my leg kept swelling and aching. Friday's game would be the last home game I'd ever play in my life, the most important of the season to many fans and to the college coaches who planned to be there scouting me.

As soon as school let out Wednesday and Thursday, I went directly home and repeated what I did before: I lay in my darkened room and, in the still and quiet, prayed to God for help. I told Him how much I loved Him and my family. I asked for relief from the pain.

The next game again came too quickly. Just before it started, I stood at attention on the field with the rest of the team for the playing of the national anthem. A steady rain poured down on us. Pain continued to shoot through my leg with the slightest movement, and even when I stood still, the inflamed muscles in my leg ached. I didn't know if any college coaches had come to the game despite the rain, and I was uncertain how well I would play, or if I even could.

As the first notes of the anthem sounded, the entire stadium grew still and quiet. It reminded me of the time I had spent praying and meditating in my still, quiet bedroom. I started praying and meditating again. A chill coursed through my body from my head to my feet, and I knew it was the Holy Spirit.

The game started, and all pain was blocked out of my body. I couldn't even hear anything. I could see people cheering and players getting physical and grunting and huffing, but the whole stadium was silent, like a movie with the sound turned off. In prayer, I cried out my thanks to God and told Him how much I loved Him.

Near the end of the first quarter, I felt as though I were being lifted in the air. I floated higher and higher. I could see my body playing on the field, but I was above it, looking down. I floated forty to fifty feet above my body. I could see everything going on in the stands and on the field in complete silence. I felt enveloped by the most intense peace and joy I had ever experienced before—or have since. I realized I was having an out-of-body experience and believed God was giving me a glimpse of heaven. I didn't want to leave. I was in the sky for the last three quarters of the game.

I played the best game of my life, sacking the quarterback six times. Up until the last play of the game, our team was tied with the opposing team, but then one of their guys threw a long ball, and another kicked a field goal to take the victory.

I slowly descended and settled back into my body, pain returning. As I walked to the locker room with my team, other players lamented the game and expressed how upset they were about our loss, but I took my helmet off, looked up to the heavens, and said, "God, never let me forget this for as long as I live."

Awed by the experience, I kept thinking, *God gave me a glimpse of heaven. If that is what heaven is like, I want to go there now. I don't want to suffer through life here and have to go through all of this pain and hurt.*

I knew how completely God loved me. The out-of-body experience had confirmed it.

I also knew that I couldn't take any credit for what had just occurred on the field. A guy would need supernatural strength to overcome the injury I had and play a game like that. I had never played that well when I was healthy and strong. It was accomplished through God's strength, not mine.

After the game, I heard that a coach from Wayne State College had been there and said he had never seen anybody in high school play as well as I did in that game. Other coaches didn't make the game, and there was no footage because rain blurred the camera lens. Coaches from the University of Nebraska came to my next game, my last one, and I played well, but not as well as I had when I was wracked with pain but uplifted by God. Coaches Tom Osborne and Lou Holtz recruited me, but they wanted me to come to the college team as a walk-on.

With the season over, I won all kinds of awards, making all-conference and being voted first team all-state. The year before, I had never even made all-conference. The *Norfolk Daily News* named me the top player of any-sized school in their distribution area, which covered about a third of the state—all the way from north of Omaha to up past Valentine. The *Omaha World-Herald* put me down as all-state, class-C defensive end. All I could say was, "Wow."

It was ego boosting, but I knew that it happened only because God had let me go through what I did. If I had been healthy and strong, I would never have been able to play that well. I went on to play for Morningside College in Sioux City, Iowa, but I never had a game like that again. But I will always remember how when I was weak, God was strong.

Waiting for Justice

Steven Thompson

"However, when the Son of Man comes, will he find faith on the earth?" (Luke 18:8) was a passage from Scripture that I never understood during my three decades of Bible study. I never knew why Jesus had asked that particular question until I faced some unwanted legal problems.

I went through several months of negotiations before the final outcome was to be determined in court. I had hoped for an amicable agreement, but the court appearance was only three days away, and no solution had been found yet.

When the problem had first surfaced several months earlier, I told a close friend about it because my anger and frustration deeply affected my objectivity. My strong Christian friend based his decisions on biblical concepts, and I believed he could provide the objectivity that was hard for me to find. We spent several meetings discussing the matter and praying about it. Over time we concluded I should follow scriptural mandates that focused on loving and forgiving our enemies and turning the other cheek. Since I'd been betrayed, this wasn't easy for me.

God instructs us in 1 Corinthians 6:1–7 not to battle in court with a fellow Christian, even when they initiate the legal proceedings. Following these instructions meant I had to trust God for justice in the matter instead of depending on my own resources to protect my monetary interests.

Thus, I gave specific instructions to my Christian lawyer: "I want you to have as little involvement as possible in these legal matters."

I only sought his services to guide me through the unavoidable legal maze that had been forced upon me. I realized I needed his legal services to provide a final solution to the matter.

Because of these decisions, there wasn't much to battle over. I had cooperated in sharing the monetary funds, hoping the proceedings would be handled in a civil and amicable manner, but I discovered it would be more frustrating and public than I had expected.

My caring lawyer had followed my request and spent most of his time replying to the other party's requests and informing me of the next steps in the process. But during the final months before the settlement, I realized my lawyer had been asked to help draw up some of the legal papers for the final settlement.

I reminded him that this matter was the plaintiff's, and he could not be involved in any of the legal drafts. My lawyer followed my wishes and contacted the other attorney, placing the drafting of the final document in his hands.

As time progressed, others encouraged me to defend my interests more aggressively. It was difficult to stay committed to biblical principles because my passive approach was costing me financially. It seemed the more I surrendered, the more they requested. It became difficult to turn the other cheek because I felt I was allowing myself to be a doormat. I began to wonder if I was being foolish and if I should have listened to those who had advised me to take a stronger stand.

A few nights before the final settlement, I paced around my house, frustrated, wondering if choosing God's way had been a wise decision. I had tried to follow biblical instructions, but I hadn't noticed any benefit. I felt I was being exploited.

I wondered if my motives were as honorable as I had thought, because I had believed God would perform an eleventh-hour miracle in payment for my obedience. I had hoped He would soften the other party's heart and that there would be some kind of reconciliation. I had reasoned that if the other party wouldn't soften, then surely God could apply enough pressure to force them to resolve the matter.

"Don't you care about justice, God? I have done what your Word says, and it seems the other party just profits from it. Does a person have to wait to get justice in heaven? Is there no justice on this earth?" I cried out to God.

Still frustrated, I pulled out my concordance to see what God's Word said about justice. I first encountered a stern rebuke from the Old Testament: "You have wearied the Lord with your words. 'How have we wearied him?' you ask. By saying, 'All who do evil are good in the eyes of the Lord, and he is pleased with them' or 'Where is the God of justice?'" (Malachi 2:17).

Often those very thoughts had traveled through my mind, and I had to confess my sin of cynicism before the Lord.

I continued searching the concordance for New Testament passages on justice and soon came to Luke 18:1–8. I had read this passage, which tells the story of a widow seeking justice, and had heard numerous sermons on it, but all the teachings had emphasized the truth that we need to persevere in prayer and not quit.

Now for the first time I noticed Luke 18:1–8 not only was about prayer, but also put a strong emphasis on seeking earthly justice. I was surprised by a promise that Jesus gave to His disciples while telling the parable: "And will not God bring about justice for his chosen ones, who cry out to him day and night? Will he keep putting them off? I tell you, he will see that they get justice, and quickly. However, when the Son of Man comes, will he find faith on the earth?" (Luke 18:7–8).

Armed with that promise, I hoped the upcoming proceedings would bring some sort of miraculous justice, but three days later, when the final settlement was signed, there was no evidence of it. Having my hope crushed again, I was confused and wondered why God had allowed me to find the promise and why it had spoken so deeply to my heart.

A few days later, I discovered a final draft of the signed settlement in my mailbox. Dejected, I left it sealed because I had signed the document the week before. I was glad the whole ordeal was over and figured opening the envelope would just incite negative memories. It was several more days before I opened the legal document and read it.

I was shocked and frustrated when I finally took the time to read it. I had heavily relied on my lawyer's advice and had never studied the document closely until now. I had only requested that my lawyer protect one point of interest throughout the proceedings, and now, studying the final agreement, I felt I had been taken advantage of in that area as well, and I was upset.

I quickly phoned my lawyer. I asked why he had failed to defend the only request I had made of him. He responded by saying I was misinterpreting the legal terminology in the final draft. He pointed out that the document drawn up by the other party had, for some reason, given me an advantage in the settlement.

"Why would they do that?" I asked.

"I don't know," he replied.

Hanging up the phone, I realized God had kept His promise for earthly justice. For whatever reason, the language in the document, which was produced by the opposition, had provided me enough of an advantage that it almost paid for my legal fees.

Not only was I awed by how God had provided justice, but I finally understood Jesus' question in Luke 18:8: "However, when the Son of Man comes, will he find faith on the earth?"

Some people say the toughest area of life to trust God with is justice. It is easier for believers to trust God for finances, health, and relationships than to trust Him for personal protection and earthly justice. We believers are prone to either fight our own battles or surrender to injustice, reasoning that God will take care of all injustices during the final judgment.

Whenever I say the Lord's Prayer, I am reminded of God challenging us to pray for justice in the situations we face: "Thy kingdom come, Thy will be done in earth, as it is in heaven" (Matthew 6:10 KJV).

If there is true justice in heaven, as most believers say there will be, then we need to pray for it on earth, as well.

Jesus' question found in Luke 18:8 should challenge all Christians to believe that God will still provide earthly justice for all of His children who will earnestly pray and trust Him for it.

Mama's Kiss

Barbara Wells

When she could no longer live in her home, we were all heartbroken. Mama loved being a homemaker. She was fun loving, outgoing, and hospitable. Friends and family would sit around her table, drinking coffee or soda pop. The radio would be playing country music. She always wanted to serve visitors a piece of the cake she had just baked—my favorite was her yellow cake with thick caramel icing. Every summer she canned vegetables—corn, pickles, tomato juice. My dad had to build shelves along an entire wall in the pantry to hold all the jars. Mama liked to sew her own curtains for the kitchen windows. Then she would sew a matching tablecloth. I remember the backyard fence was covered with pink country roses. We also had a gazebo with white, pink, yellow, and crimson roses cascading to the ground. I loved going in there and reading books from the school library. I could go all over the world and still be home for supper when Mama called me to come inside.

Everybody who knew her loved her, especially her six children. She had four boys and two girls. She was our cheerleader, always encouraging us to get involved in school and church activities. I can remember her always saying, "Life is for the living." I believe she learned that from the way she grew up.

Her mother became ill and passed away when Mama had just turned thirteen. She had to quit school and take care of her four younger siblings. Her dad worked in the coal mines—she really was a coal miner's daughter. Those emotionally hard times certainly helped to develop her appreciation for life, friends, and family.

My dad always called Mama "the heart of the home." I really think she and Daddy were the wind beneath each other's wings. They were a committed team. About two years after his retirement, my dad's health began declining. One fall he became ill with pneumonia, was hospitalized, and died of congestive heart failure.

In the last years of Mama's life, she began having mini-strokes. During a major surgery, she experienced a massive stroke, which left her paralyzed and unable to speak clearly. Following a short time of speech therapy, she could mumble yes and no and attempt singing a few lines of "Amazing Grace."

Mama had to have total care and was confined to a wheelchair. It was sad to watch her zest for life fade. We all helped transition her to a special nursing facility that could address her level of care requirements. Mama's new home was lovely; some of her friends also lived there. Because she could sit in a wheelchair a few hours a day, she was able to attend many activities provided by the staff. Mama was always all about us before her illness; now we experienced a role reversal. We started taking care of her. Because I became her official caregiver, I attended all monthly plan-of-care meetings, which included her social worker and all department heads. They reviewed her medical needs and her social interests. I discussed the family's observations and her doctor's input.

Our visits were wonderful bonding times. Fridays she went to the beauty shop to have her hair styled; then I pushed her wheelchair to a small restaurant next door to the facility. We sat at a table and drank coffee. We shared lunch. Her strength only lasted for short periods of time. Every time I stopped by, Mama would smile and kiss me.

The time came when she could no longer get out of bed. She slept a lot and lost her appetite. The doctor hospitalized her. Within two days she passed away peacefully, with all her children at her bedside.

The day she passed away, I visited her room and heard her calling out, "Ma! Ma!" I realized she was talking to her mother, who had passed away when my mother was just a young teenager, over seventy years earlier. I knew she was leaving and was very quiet so I would not interrupt what was taking place. I believe she was seeing her mother and calling her name, completely unaware of my presence. It was a great honor to be with her in those final moments and bear witness to the heavenly reunion between my mother and the grandmother I never got to meet.

Almost a year had passed since Mama died. Every time I saw a wheelchair, my heart would feel the same broken sadness.

But one night I had a dream that brought such happiness and peace to me and has never left me. In the dream, I saw Mama. She was young, about thirty. Her hair wasn't white anymore, but a beautiful auburn brown again. She wasn't in a wheelchair. She was walking through a beautiful garden of windswept field flowers of every color. She walked right up to me, her brown eyes smiling, and she leaned over and kissed me directly on my left cheek.

I awoke to the ring of the alarm clock. It was Sunday morning—time to get up. I could almost smell her buffet breakfast.

I believe God gave me the dream to heal my broken heart and let me see that Mama is happy and healthy and home with God.

Breath of God

FRAN CAFFEY SANDIN

At three in the morning, most people in the Dallas–Fort Worth area were asleep, but my eyes were locked on the ambulance traveling in front of me. I couldn't let it out of sight because I didn't know the directions to Cook Children's hospital in Fort Worth. My foot pressed hard on the accelerator as I glanced at the speedometer—ninety miles per hour. I drove my blue Volvo sedan faster as needed.

Our young adult son, Steve, was being transferred from an Irving hospital emergency room due to difficulty breathing and dangerously low hemoglobin. Through the dim light in the back window I saw Steve—propped up on the gurney, receiving oxygen by mask. Between the speed and the adrenaline, I felt the Lord's presence in the passenger's seat beside me, and His Spirit was comforting.

We arrived quickly, and I found the ER parking area. The medical personnel were ready and waiting for the ambulance. An antiseptic aroma surrounded me as I entered the double doors to the ER, where doctors and nurses were already working. Within minutes, Steve was transferred to the ICU for further treatment.

Steve had been diagnosed with cystic fibrosis a few years earlier at the age of twenty-nine. He had just completed a master of physical therapy degree and was working as a physical therapist at Arlington Memorial Hospital when he contracted pneumonia and became a patient himself. His doctor, who had previously treated CF patients, said, “Steve, I think you have cystic fibrosis.”

My husband and I were shocked, as no one else in our family had the genetic disease. As a boy, Steve had allergies and occasional bouts of bronchitis. We had him tested and treated with allergy shots. When in college he required surgery to remove nasal polyps, but he was not the typical CF patient. Strong and muscular, he was a gifted athlete, the star player on his high school basketball team, and a winner of swim team awards. Steve had good nutrition, always worked out, did not drink alcohol, and didn’t use tobacco products. He was six feet two and weighed about 190 pounds. When the doctor explained the disease, he said, “Steve, you have done everything right.”

Two positive sweat tests confirmed the diagnosis. As a physical therapist, Steve had learned how to treat patients with cystic fibrosis but never dreamed he would become his own caregiver. He began respiratory treatments four times a day with medications to liquify the thick secretions in his lungs, which provided a perfect medium for bacterial and fungal infections.

Shortly thereafter, Steve developed symptoms that prompted his doctor to run further tests. He learned he also had IgA nephropathy, an autoimmune disease affecting the kidneys. About 75 percent of people with that disease go on to live a normal life, but 25 percent progress to renal failure. Steve was in the second group and required hemodialysis three times a week. His double diagnosis became extremely complicated as he had two difficult diseases in his body that were fighting each other. With CF he needed lots of liquids; with kidney failure and dialysis he needed restricted fluids. With CF he needed a high caloric intake; with dialysis he had a diminished appetite and food didn't taste the same. Juggling all the details became a huge problem, but Steve was amazing and brilliant at taking care of himself.

Steve subsequently moved to Irving, Texas, and worked as a therapist for a home health agency to accommodate his complex schedule of lung treatments and dialysis.

That's when he got a severe infection and was transferred to Cook Children's in Fort Worth because his CF clinic was located there. Steve had an extended hospital stay.

When I walked into the ICU room, Steve was pale, and he was sitting on the side of his bed, receiving supplemental oxygen, and leaning on a pillow placed on the over-bed table. My heart sank. Friends and family were praying for Steve and for me, or I wouldn't have made it through the day. Steve spent many days receiving IV antibiotics and blood transfusions, but he finally began to improve and regain strength.

Everyone was really nice, attentive, and efficient at the children's hospital, but when Steve started improving, he said with a cute grin, "Mom, I'm feeling better, but I'm really tired of these Happy Meals." So I enjoyed taking him downstairs for some real man food at the grill. Finally, after he was released, I continued to stay with him at his Irving townhouse until he could manage alone. We often watched lighthearted reruns of *I Love Lucy*, *The Beverly Hillbillies*, *Mayberry R.F.D.*, *The Andy Griffith Show*, and others that gave us a reason to laugh together. Although my husband, Jim, and

I lived in Greenville, about an hour east of the metroplex, Steve wanted to maintain his Irving residence to be near his doctors and continue his work.

After three years, Steve wanted to try peritoneal dialysis so he could dialyze at his home instead of driving to the clinic three times a week. He had a peritoneal catheter inserted, and after a few initial problems, it worked well for him. He received a Fresenius dialysis machine to use at his townhouse. Each month a truck driver delivered boxes of dialysis fluid and the necessary supplies. After a few instructions, Steve could take care of his dialysis with regular checkups at the Grapevine DaVita clinic.

Steve really enjoyed his profession, and his patients appreciated his kind, gentle manner and his ability to teach exercises and explain how to take better care of themselves. Steve was conscientious and sometimes worked when he was sicker than his patients.

With peritoneal dialysis, Steve had more freedom with his schedule, so we invited him to go with us on a few trips. It took some advance planning, but Fresenius delivered a dialysis machine and the supplies for dialysis to our hotel destination, and an oxygen concentrator delivered separately helped Steve at night. He could go about six hours without nebulizer lung treatments, and that gave us time to drive or fly to our destinations.

So for four years, Jim, Steve, and I enjoyed trips to San Antonio and Albuquerque, New Mexico. Jim and I let Steve set the pace, and we had some wonderful, special times together.

When Steve no longer had the energy to work part-time, he began a home-based business using his computer to sell air purifiers. He started receiving orders from across the US. With the local post office just down the street, he conveniently mailed the items.

Steve had received Christ as his Savior at the age of eight and faithfully participated in Bible studies throughout his high school and college years. He did not complain about his situation, but when he attended church he often asked for prayer, and many, many people prayed with and for him. Each time we were together, we prayed. Since we know that "with God, all things are possible" (Matthew 19:26), we prayed for healing.

In 2008–2009 Steve endured ten hospitalizations in thirteen months. During that time while he was recovering at home, the Lord gave him a project. He wrote two books: *Jesus Really Said It* and *Make the Right Choice*, which is based on the book of Proverbs. We were delighted and surprised when he showed us his published work.

I drove to Steve's townhouse in Irving one day a week to help with laundry, cleaning, grocery shopping, and whatever else Steve needed. Whenever he felt like it, I took him out to lunch and we enjoyed some meaningful conversations. One day in 2012 he said, "Mom, you know I've been sick a really long time." His weight had gradually dropped to 140, and he was visibly weaker and a shadow of his former self.

I answered, "I know, Steve, but God will not take you home until your work on earth is done."

Only a few days later, Steve called to say, "Mom, I have done everything I know to do, but I'm not able to breathe well. I think I need IV antibiotics."

Grabbing my bag, already packed and ready to go since I was always on call, I drove to Irving. I took Steve to the hospital, along with his peritoneal dialysis machine and all the supplies for his dialysis. After the first few days, Steve seemed to improve.

Some friends from Steve's church came to visit. On a Sunday afternoon, two young ladies brought the Communion elements and a guitar. They sang worship songs and shared Communion with Steve. It meant the world to him and to me. On another occasion, his pastor and church elders came, anointed him with oil, and prayed specifically for his healing.

But God had other plans. Steve took a turn for the worse. He lost the feeling in his hands and could not walk. He knew something was happening, but he was unable to stop it. He suffered from excruciating pain in his legs. Later we learned it was infectious vasculitis. The antibiotics could no longer hold back the infections from his body.

He closed his eyes and whispered, "Jesus, Jesus." Tears rolled down his cheeks. I hugged him and told him I loved him.

When he entered ICU for the last time, I could only think of the song "Breath of Heaven (Mary's Song)" by Amy Grant. In it Mary asks the Breath of Heaven, the Lord, to be near her.

"Hold me together, Breath of Heaven," I prayed. I felt God was telling me that Steve would be going to heaven. When I drove home one day to pick up some fresh clothes and rest for a few hours, I could only cry, pray, and sing that song. On September 22, 2012, at the age of forty-three, Steve, transported by angels, passed peacefully from this earth and began breathing the breath of heaven.

About two weeks later, my dear friend Jeanette, from San Antonio, invited me to attend a women's conference with her. One night while I was there, God gave me a dream almost as vivid as a vision. It was Steve, dressed in a suit, healthy, well-nourished, muscular, and smiling as he declared, "Mom, I'm well!"

It was so real I could have reached out to touch him. What a blessing!

Then some time later, I was sleeping at home and awoke to the strong fragrance of fresh flowers. Once Steve had sent a bouquet with a thoughtful note: "Mom, thank you for taking care of me." I felt like Steve had sent flowers from heaven. It was another gift from the Lord.

More recently I had been studying Revelation and had another dream. In my dream, I was at Steve's townhouse when I heard a car drive into the garage. It was Steve and our son-in-law, Beau. The back door flew open and Steve, joyful, dressed in a white robe, came toward me with his arms extended and exclaimed, "Mom, I'm alive!" He gave me a big hug, and the dream ended.

I felt like singing. Then I recalled reading what Jesus said: "I am the resurrection and the life. He who believes in Me, though he may die, he shall live. And whoever lives and believes in Me shall never die" (John 11:25–26 NKJV).

My experiences after Steve's move to heaven reminded me of a quote by the late Peter Marshall, a former US Senate chaplain: "Those we love are with the Lord, . . . and the Lord has promised to be with us. . . . If they are with Him, and He is with us . . . *they cannot be far away*."*

*Peter Marshall, *Mr. Jones, Meet the Master* (New York: Revell, 1949, 1950), 171.

He Miraculously Vanished!

SANDRA L. HICKMAN

At the house beside the sea, we often felt as though we were disciples of old. We felt like the New Testament Twelve dwelling with Jesus by the Sea of Galilee. Yet we were just ordinary people in coastal Western Australia following the extraordinary Savior.

The smell of the ocean and the sound of the waves and the gusty, salty wind were our constant backdrop. The sun shone brightly over blue waters glistening with whitecaps. Come evening, the stars would light up the indigo sky over dark, brooding waters, as if displaying the more serious side and preeminence of our Maker. Even the moon had a serious face.

The scene seemed constantly set for something godly to come crashing into our world. Indeed, the blessings of God did crash into our world as we held prayer meetings, home-group meetings, and even some Sunday home-church meetings. Everyone would gather, bringing refreshments, coming always with their Bibles and musical instruments. The little ones were always well behaved in the playroom and the back garden, and sometimes they joined in with us in the most glorious, unexpected ways.

We witnessed the presence of God in our children. They were such innocent blank canvases upon which the Holy Spirit could paint amazing scenes of worship and love to the Lord as we sat in reverence of Him.

It was such a surreal time in our lives—we almost felt like Jesus would come walking in at any moment. Truly, Jesus was very present all throughout our many meetings; we often felt as though we were sitting at His feet. The Holy Spirit anointing always dwelt heavily in that house.

My daughter Tari and her three young children, Jordan, Eligh, and Isabella were so happy living there. Tari was merely renting the house, but it felt like home. A lovely set of French doors opened out onto the front garden. On warm evenings, we opened the doors, and our worship music filled the air. Sometimes passersby would stop and listen. It was a season of God when we lived in a bubble of heavenly anointing.

There were so many amazing occurrences; most were good, but some were not so good. We were certainly challenged by "he who is in the world" (1 John 4:4 NKJV). But God was so very evident, and God prevailed and presided over that place. It was His house.

I recall one particular incident that brought conviction and proof of how God works to reveal His presence. That day the sun was shining, and the smell of summer hung in the air. Just Tari and Jordan were at home, where Jordan was homeschooled due to his cerebral palsy. The younger children had gone to school.

Tari and I were chatting on our mobile phones when she realized something. "Oh, Mom, I've left my handbag in the car, and I'm not sure if it's locked. I'd better go check."

We continued chatting as she walked outside. She reached into the car, grabbed her handbag, and turned, and she was startled to see a man standing at the back of the car, staring at her. He was in his late twenties. He was dressed in shabby, dirty clothes, had straggly, messy hair, and had a cigarette resting behind one ear. His sudden presence really scared Tari.

She was glad she had her phone in her hand and to know I was listening in. The man asked, "Can you give me some water? I'm thirsty; can you fill this up for me?"

He held up an empty, stubby beer bottle. Thinking quickly, she spoke into her phone, "Hang on, Mom, there's a man here, and he wants me to give him some water. I'm going inside to get it. Just wait; hold on . . ." I could sense fear in her voice.

Tari saw that the man was now standing between her and the front door of the house. She bravely walked past him, taking the bottle, knowing that he was following her. She told him to wait outside by the door, which she locked as she went in.

By now I was feeling very uneasy. I warned, "Keep that door locked!"

She placed her phone on a small table inside the living room near the front door before proceeding to the kitchen. I knew she wanted this man to understand that I was on the phone, listening and knowing he was there. In a hoarse whisper she instructed Jordan to stay away from the door. I was hanging on the other end of the phone, trying to listen, praying in earnest silence.

She later recounted that once in the kitchen, she entered into a struggle with God. "Lord, I don't want to open my front door again. I am afraid of his intentions. What if he pushes his way into the house? He might rob us, and what about Jordan? And what might he do to me?"

She was imagining every terrible scenario! The Holy Spirit quieted her, bringing to her mind two Scriptures—one about giving a cup of water to someone, and the other about not forgetting to entertain strangers, because they might be angels. As she debated with God, she again heard the Holy Spirit saying not to judge by appearances. She had entered the kitchen in her fearful flesh, judging this man by his appearance, looking at everything she was afraid of. Once she allowed herself to actually listen to the Holy Spirit, she knew what she must do. She felt God wanted to bless her, and only she could rob herself of receiving those blessings by disobedience.

So my daughter did give that man the water he asked for. However, as she was about to fill the small beer bottle, she heard the Holy Spirit say, "Use cold water from the refrigerator." So that's what she did. But she decided to give the man extra water, so she took a large, clean plastic bottle and filled it to the top with the cold water and walked to the front door. That's when everything changed.

"You won't believe this, Mom."

Believe what? My mind was racing!

"When I handed him the bottle of water, I saw something I didn't see before. It was as though I was seeing his eyes for the first time. They were beautiful. I couldn't stop looking into them. Peace flooded over me, and I was completely at ease. All fear vanished as I looked into his eyes. They were so blue. The most perfect color of blue I've ever seen. I felt such peace and love. I said to him, 'Here is the water. God bless you in Jesus' name.' He looked directly at me and replied, 'No . . . God bless you!'" Tari excitedly declared, "I know this was no ordinary man. I don't think he even was a man. I think he was an angel."

I held the phone in my hand, flabbergasted as she continued speaking. "Mom," she said, her voice so peaceful, yet filled with astonishment, "he took the bottle; then as I watched, he turned, took two steps, and disappeared in front of me! He simply vanished. I . . . I could barely believe my eyes! I yelled for Jordan to come!"

Incredulously, I said to her, "He just disappeared? You didn't see him go in any direction?"

"No, Mom, I watched him walk two steps from me and vanish!" I knew in my spirit that something unique had just occurred. Had she really seen an angel? I needed to be there.

"Tari, I'm coming over. I'm leaving now."

We sat and talked, analyzing every aspect of this occurrence. She spoke about how the man looked as though he'd been out all night on a drunken bender. How the driveway leading to the house was long, making it impossible for anyone to appear in the carport that quickly. How her car was parked right alongside the front door, making it a few seconds to get to the house from the car. And yet in just a second or two he appeared there. Then he miraculously vanished before her eyes!

We rejoiced and praised God. We both knew in our spirits that it was true. It was a heavenly visitation!

Tari told me with renewed confidence and wisdom, "God knew if He sent someone, even an angel in disguise, for me to totally trust Him beyond any fear, it would have to be someone I would feel comfortable with. Like a girl or a woman or even an elderly gentleman. Someone perhaps looking for directions, knocking on doors, doing surveys . . . but God chose to send someone I would instantly be wary of. The very look of him made him the type of person I would never want to confront. The Lord was testing me to see if I would give a thirsty stranger a drink of water on a hot day, regardless of how he looked!"

As we sat reveling in the truth of what she'd witnessed, we were astounded and amazed. We remembered how Jesus had spoken in the Bible about giving a cup of water (Matthew 10:42), but we had forgotten He said it was to be a cup of *cold* water! And how the Holy Spirit had said exactly that to Tari, "Use *cold* water from the refrigerator." Such a small, yet imperative detail proving the precision of God and His Word!

Just about two weeks before all this occurred, Tari had been reading a book on people's experiences of seeing angels and divine visitations. She had thought how wonderful that would be. She wondered if that could ever happen to her. She pondered it while talking to God. And God surely answered.

I believe God was testing my daughter and teaching her at the same time. Testing to see if she would do what she knew was right according to His Word. Teaching her that no matter how scary the stranger at her door appears, all she has to do is trust God! And who knows if it might even have been the Angel of the Lord. The same One who appeared to Abraham, Joseph, and many others.

Defying the Laws of Physics

Jan Apilado

How drastically our lives had changed!

Just one week. That's all the time it had taken for God's miraculous transition to take place—one that changed our direction and our lives forever.

After my husband and I had spent more than twenty years in the wholesale gift industry, the Lord drew us to a new career, and my husband's first step was to attend seminary. We had no doubt that this was God's call on our lives. He threw open every door. He overcame every obstacle to His plan. We felt His peace every step of the way because we had no doubt that He was leading us.

On his first day of class, my dear husband, Corky, sat there in total confusion. His mind spun as he struggled to understand exactly how he had gone so suddenly from being a businessman to being a Bible student. He'd not been in a classroom for more than thirty years. As his mind filled with doubts, he asked himself, *What was I thinking?*

Then he wondered how he could ever manage the challenge of graduate-level courses.

But he calmed himself as he remembered this was where God had placed him.

Since these changes had come upon us so quickly, I was responsible for arranging the dissolving of our sales firm. Corky and I had agreed that we would not sell our company—instead, we wanted to give it to our sales staff. After phoning our employees with our news, I told them that if our importers agreed, they would now be the primary reps in their territories. Then I informed our importers of the big changes, and all but one of them agreed to let our salespeople represent them.

Then I needed to find a job, and I needed one soon. Before the Lord changed our lives, we had just completed the gift shows for the new fall and Christmas merchandise. So we were concerned about paying off our travel expenses. Our credit cards were close to being maxed out. But no commission checks on those sales would be coming for three to four months.

Since God had worked out all the other details for us, we put finding me the right job in His hands, too. He had already provided for Corky's tuition and books through a dear Christian couple. A week after we had told them of God's plan for us, they informed us that God had called them to pledge a monthly donation to cover the cost of seminary. They were far from wealthy, so we were both humbled and grateful for their obedience to God and their help.

Since our home is in a small rural community more than thirty miles from Portland, Oregon, very few jobs were available locally. I'd likely be driving many miles on our winding country roads, so I focused my job search on areas closest to us. My second interview was for the position of office manager for a construction company. Managing our small business had given me the experience they required in bookkeeping, tax filing, and on occasion, offering advice on employee problems.

I was hired. That was the place God had for me, and I soon became a "mom" to forty roofers, because roofing is a young man's job.

I loved my job, and both bosses were great. They operated with good values and were generous to their employees. My first year with them flew by without any serious travel problems, even though the first twenty miles of my daily commute were on very narrow, curvy roads. I was apprehensive about driving every day. Corky loved driving, so he drove nearly all the time during our business travels. He had a wonderful sense of direction, never getting lost, while I have none, get lost easily, and become nervous over hazardous conditions.

My second winter, however, was a bit more challenging. The Pacific Northwest experienced more icy mornings than normal and many snow days. But my little front-wheel-drive car handled those conditions quite well. Being responsible for payroll doesn't allow you to stay home just because the weather is nasty. And when the weather was bad, while I waited for the car to warm up, I always asked God for His shield of protection.

One week in January, the thermometer had not read above freezing for five days, and that morning's temperature was 18 degrees Fahrenheit. I left for work early that day, knowing it would be a difficult commute. And it was. As I drove the three miles of side road to access the main road, I saw that three cars had skidded off the road and been abandoned.

My prayers continued as I cautiously kept driving. I asked God for better conditions as I reached the stop sign before the main paved road. This road would eventually lead me to the highway. It seemed strange to me that so few drivers were on the road. I decided that either many others were smarter than I and had decided not to tackle the drive, or perhaps they'd tried the drive, given up, and headed back for home and a nice warm fire.

After smoothly maneuvering several steep hills, I came to the series of tight twenty-five- and thirty-mile-per-hour curves. When I approached the first posted twenty-five-mile-per-hour curve, I could not believe my eyes! Suddenly, coming straight at me was a huge dump truck, fully loaded with gravel. The driver appeared to be out of control and was in half of my lane. On my right was the high stone bank that had been blasted to make the roadway. I had no place to go!

But, surprisingly, I felt no panic, and no fear overcame me. God's gentle calm enveloped me.

Calmly, I closed my eyes while my hands remained steady on the steering wheel. My words were, "Okay, Lord, if this is my time to go home to you, I'm ready."

It seemed an eternity, but I know it was only seconds later that I opened my eyes to see in my rearview mirror that big dump truck, now behind me, still traveling in half of my lane.

The only explanation is that God passed me through that truck. There is no other way we could have avoided a horrible crash. As I passed through that truck, God's calm and His peace surrounded me and flowed through me. I felt only His love.

I'm unable to find and incapable to describe by mere words how I felt the Lord's covering and His presence. And I can feel it again now, almost as incredibly, as I share with you the experience of His miracle on that day. The day that God defied the laws of physics just for me, His child.

He Met Me in My Mess

Kelly J. Stigliano

"You're ridiculous to even *think* you can relate to that woman!"

I couldn't believe what I was reading. While the communication between my former husband and me was intermittent, he still tried to abuse me through the US mail. Admittedly, words in letters didn't leave bruises like the ones he had given me while we were together, but they hurt nonetheless.

This was one of the few times I looked forward to my daughter and son growing up. It was 1984, and they were both preschoolers.

"After they can write for themselves, I won't have to correspond with him at all," I told a friend.

With seven states between us, I felt it was my responsibility to send their painted and colored pictures to their daddy and to read his letters to them. Knowing I'd be the reader, he often sandwiched sarcasm between the lines for my benefit.

Certainly, small children couldn't understand phrases like "Don't let the dregs of society drag you down."

I usually included a note from me with their artwork, updating him on what the kids were doing and occasionally making small talk. I'd stopped begging for child support months earlier—it did no good. He had no intention of pitching in financially. I learned this from his written comments: "So the kids need new shoes, huh? Well, what's new? As soon as I find the money tree, I'll share some with you."

In his responses, he often tried to belittle me by putting the pronunciations and meanings of words in parentheses, insinuating I was unable to understand his vocabulary. It was his attempt to wield power over me from afar.

I continued to read his words. "I never punched you and never sent you to the hospital. You're delusional (di loo′ zhun al—a false belief or opinion that is contrary to fact or reality)."

There was a time when I believed him. As a brainwashed wife, I'd thought that if a fist wasn't involved, it wasn't really wife beating. Despite a chipped tooth, bloody head, and bruises, I wasn't to feel like a victim.

However, there was now enough space and time between us for my mind to clear, and I realized that wasn't true. Mistreatment can come in a variety of forms. Slapping, choking, kicking, or closed-fist punching—it was all abusive.

The Burning Bed, a television movie starring Farrah Fawcett, had aired a couple of weeks earlier. It was based on a true story about Francine Hughes, an abused wife who killed her husband. I found it terrifying and somewhat relatable.

I'd asked my ex-husband in a letter if he'd seen it. In his reply, he ridiculed the movie and me.

It was true that he had never struck me with his fist. It was also true that I'd never been hospitalized.

However, Francine Hughes stayed with her husband for more than ten years. I left my husband before our fifth wedding anniversary. Who knows what might have happened if I'd stayed? Bruises can lead to broken bones. Choking and kicking can lead to hospital visits—or worse.

Furthermore, for years I'd prayed for God to kill him or give me courage to do it myself. I just wanted my misery to end and didn't think I could escape alive. I secretly envied Hughes's courage to murder her husband, as portrayed in the film.

Now I was sorry I'd asked him if he'd watched the movie. As I read his mocking response, old wounds opened again. The letter sat in my lap as flashbacks of his physical attacks on me pervaded my thoughts.

Life for my children and me was so wonderfully different now, since the divorce. My ex-husband lived two thousand miles away. My parents had bought us a single-wide mobile home in the country. It was perfect for the three of us. Everything was new, and we were healing and adapting nicely.

I had been taking my daughter and son to church and Sunday school each week. I read my Bible daily, and we prayed together every night. Although I'd previously struggled with alcohol, I hadn't had a drink in over a year—didn't even want one.

I was finally being the mother God wanted me to be. We had friends at church and enjoyed visits with my family, something my ex-husband had never allowed. My kids were happy. I loved our life as a joyful little trio and the direction we were going.

Then I saw the commercial. *The Burning Bed* was going to be on television again the following weekend. When I heard the ad, something inside me snapped. My ex-husband's words played in a painful loop in my head. "You're ridiculous to even *think* you can relate to that woman! You're delusional."

In his denial of any wrongdoing, he tried to trivialize the horror we once called a marriage.

So I planned an evening of getting drunk while I watched the show again. It was a premeditated personal pity party.

As if in a fog, I drove to the liquor store. For the only time in my life, I left my precious children in the car while I went into a store. They sat alone in my Ford Escort with the "God Loves You" bumper sticker on the back as I bought a pint of Tanqueray gin and a bottle of tonic water. My old favorite of "Tanqueray and tonic with a twist of lemon not lime, please" was going to happen in my own home—in my renewed life.

I moved as if on autopilot as I put the kids to bed early, turned on the TV, and proceeded to drink myself into a stupor. I didn't see the entire movie. I remember lying on the carpet in the living room and being sick, with the sound of Farrah Fawcett screaming in the background.

The thin shag carpet in my living room didn't insulate the floor very well, and the cold air that circulated under our mobile home chilled my body.

As I lay there in my mess, I felt the warmth of a hug. I clearly sensed someone cradling me. It was as if arms were coming through the floor, wrapping around my shoulders, holding me tight. In my spirit, I heard the Lord say, "It's all right. I understand, and I'm here with you. It's all right—I love you."

I felt overwhelming love—unconditional love.

When I woke up it was early morning, and I was still on the floor. I could hear the children playing in their bedrooms. They always came out in the morning. This morning, however, they did not. I breathed a quick prayer of thanksgiving.

I had to get moving so they wouldn't find me in that condition. I dragged myself up. My long hair stuck to my face and neck. I quietly staggered into my bathroom, washed my face, and pulled my hair back. I crept back into the living room to clean up the mess. There was a little gin left in the bottle, and I poured it down the kitchen sink.

Without letting the kids know I was awake, I snuck into the bathroom to take a shower. My head was pounding, and my body ached. As I stood under the hot water, physically washing off the filth of the previous night's sin, I cried out to God in my spirit. In silence, consumed with shame and guilt, I wept.

How did I let Satan win? Why did I knowingly drive to the store and leave my beloved kids in the car, exposing my bumper sticker—and God—to ridicule outside the liquor store? Why did I premeditatedly get drunk? I am so, so sorry, God. I am so ashamed.

I shook with sorrow as I sobbed and leaned against the wall of the shower. No punishment would have been worse than how I felt at that moment.

And yet, He loved me still.

The condemnation I perceived was not from God. I'd lived for the evil one for years, and he wasn't giving up without a fight. I allowed the enemy to taunt me and try to convince me I was a failure and shouldn't even try to live a Christian life.

Nonetheless, God held me, forgave me, and gave me strength to fight future temptations. I haven't had a drink since.

Best of all, He has never let me forget that He met me in my mess and wrapped His warm arms completely around me while I was lying on a cold floor. He whispered into my spirit that He understood, forgave me, and loved me unconditionally.

In fact, the oft-used phrase "God will turn your mess into your message" became very real to me. He has given me opportunities to share His goodness with others—His goodness that is available to anyone at any time, in any place—even in a mess.

Safe in His Arms

Delores E. Topliff

I don't think Mom intended to attempt suicide that night. She loved her children. She just felt too hurt and overwhelmed to keep living. At least, that's what she decided late that summer evening when I was fifteen, my sister was nine, and my brother was two.

I was in our backyard weeding the vegetable garden, where I raised much of our food after Dad left. My sister and brother were close by. Without saying a word, Mom left our house and walked through our yard and then down the street behind it. I straightened my back and called after her, "Where are you going?"

She didn't answer.

"Are you going to the store?" I called again, seeing her head that direction.

"Yes," she answered, her voice vague and dreamlike. She kept walking and didn't turn our way.

But when I checked my watch in the late summer twilight, it was already past nine. The store was closed. And she didn't carry a purse or anything. Now it was dark, and she was out of sight.

What to do? Our parents' divorce was in progress. Dad was in the next town with the woman he would marry. He'd been gone most of the last few years and paid minimal support—not enough. Mom's menial job paid little.

I took my siblings inside and got them ready for bed, trying to keep things normal. Next, I found Dad's phone number and called him. "Mom's gone. Disappeared. She's been gone an hour now, she's nowhere in sight, and it's pitch black. What should I do?"

"I don't know. Call the police, I guess."

"But we're minors. They'll split us up and put us in foster homes. Won't you come?"

"Nope. I'm not getting involved in your mess."

The phone clicked, and I stared at the receiver. What *could* I do?

I saw our older neighbor's lights shining, so I knocked on his front door. "Mr. Haney, would you please help me? Mom's been upset lately, and tonight she wandered off. Said she was going to the store, but it's closed. She's not back, and it's so dark—I'm worried. Will you please help me find her?"

"I'll try. Hop in the car." He revved up his old green Chevrolet sedan.

When Dad still lived at home, he and Mom had frequent loud fights. Mom sometimes raced down the street with Dad driving after her, headlights flashing across our bedroom window and walls. Eventually, he would find her and bring her back. The younger kids were usually asleep. I'd stay in my room pretending to sleep, but I was praying. Tonight, Dad wasn't here to find her and bring her home.

Mr. Haney drove our streets for several miles in every direction. After much effort but no success, he returned to his driveway.

"I'm sorry; that's the best I can do. Have you told your dad?"

I hung my head. "Yes. He doesn't want to be involved."

"I'm sorry. I don't know what to tell you, then. It's getting late. You'd better call the police."

I hesitated. In foster homes, my sister's and brother's physical needs might be met, but their emotional ones might not. I'd heard that those kids sometimes hurt nearly as much as Mom did. I didn't want that for my sister and brother.

The Baptist church down the street had become my haven. Our parents didn't attend, yet faith became my answer. I showed up every time the doors opened and started teaching Sunday school at age fourteen.

I phoned our pastor. "Mom's been upset lately and left tonight. I called Dad, but he won't come. Our neighbor drove me around our whole area, but we can't find her. I'm not sixteen. If I call the police, I'm afraid they'll put us in foster homes. What should I do?"

"Why not call Mary?"

Mary was my Sunday school teacher, who hired me most Saturdays to clean her home. I knew she'd be willing, but she and her family were scheduled to leave at six the next morning for a vacation in Canada.

"I don't want to bother her."

"Give me a minute to think." He covered the receiver, but I heard him talk in low tones to someone else in the room.

Soon he came back. "Sit tight. I'll send someone over to stay with you."

I didn't know until years later that the person Pastor Bob talked with late that night was a policeman, the only time that gentleman stopped by for counsel. Bob had asked him, "Is that true? Would the kids be put in foster care?"

"Yes," he'd said. "Don't let that happen."

Fifteen minutes later, Mary's headlights swung into our driveway.

I rushed to meet her, relieved but embarrassed. "I told Bob not to bother you. I don't want to ruin your vacation."

She pulled me close. "Don't be silly. You know I'll come anytime. Now, tell me what's going on."

We sat down at the dining room table at around midnight. My little sister had awakened, maybe from seeing Mary's headlights through her window or from hearing a different voice in our living room. Mary's presence comforted me. We discussed strategies.

"Like it or not, your dad has to get involved."

Suddenly, we saw movement behind our house. A stark white face pressed against our backyard-facing dining room window, eyes wild and staring.

I'd never seen Mom look this frightening. She threw open our back door and dashed inside, running down the hall to gather my little brother in her arms. She stared at Mary and me for a long moment without saying a word and then slammed her bedroom door shut.

Mary and I looked at each other. I'd been studying French in high school. Mary also knew the language.

"*C'est la vie*," I said and shrugged. "Have a good trip."

"*Non, c'est la guerre*," she answered. "It's war. We'll send you postcards and pray." And she did.

Dad didn't phone, and I didn't tell Mom's parents. But I prayed and asked God what to do.

The next day, Mom told me what had happened. She had only intended to walk and think through her problems. When she left, she had no plan to harm herself. She wandered and wept, later changing directions to descend the long hill to the Columbia River.

In emotional pain, she decided it was easier to quit living than to blindly hope her life would improve. She would wade into the deep river far enough for it to carry her away so the tormenting memories and voices would stop. To reach the water she crossed railroad tracks and fought through blackberry thickets where she got badly scratched. Several dogs chased her, and she stumbled through thick, mucky sand near the water's edge before reaching the river's main channel.

She stood shaking in darkness on the north side of the river dividing Oregon and Washington. No one saw her. She saw the powerful current push everything in its path toward the ocean while her mind raced just as fast. Yes, this could work. She waded through the shallows to a sandbar. Her chest heaved. She muttered words—not so much praying as spewing emotions. "I just want everything to end. I don't want to think anymore!"

She said that at that moment one bright beam of moonlight broke through the clouds and lit the shoreline, the sandbar, and her. Eyes wide, she told me, "I heard a voice ask, 'Are you so sure this is all there is and that you won't have to meet me?'"

She could not answer. She just stood there trembling as she realized that God knew her thoughts, and she was not ready to face Him. Before long, she retraced her steps—back through the shallows, through the thick, sludge-like sand. Crossing over the railroad tracks and through thick blackberry brambles, she got more scratched and muddier still. She fought her way past the yapping dogs again and trudged up our long hill.

Seeing Mary's car in our driveway, Mom looked through our window to see what was happening inside before she rushed in.

Nothing had changed, except Mom did survive. I thought I was shielding my sister and brother from Mom's instability, but the next day she screamed and squeezed her own throat tightly in front of us until her eyes bulged.

Later my nine-year-old sister asked me, "Should we talk to our pastor? Or a doctor? Or a psychologist?"

She was fully aware. I wasn't shielding her or my brother from anything. Something had to be done.

Mom had hoped to go to college to become a nurse but never had the chance. At her current job in a potato chip factory, she had slipped on spilled oil and fallen on the concrete floor and hurt her back. Other fill-in jobs also involved food processing. At a cookie manufacturer, she literally faced out-of-control cookie filling like in that famous *I Love Lucy* episode.

I prayed harder than ever and began to hear a plan. I was to give Mom an ultimatum involving safe boundaries and opportunities for all of us—or I would contact the judge overseeing the divorce and get custody of the kids myself. I didn't know I was too young for that to happen. But because I believed I could do it, I was convincing.

Still, I sat on my bed, quaking, working up the courage to face Mom because she often dished out physical abuse. God impressed on me that I only had to take the first step. He would help me take every next one.

I found her primping in the bathroom. "Mom, you should rent out this house to pay the mortgage and move in with your mom and dad. They can take care of the kids, so you can go to college and become a nurse like you've dreamed. But give me my freedom to go where I want, or I'll go to the judge granting your divorce and get custody of the kids myself. I'll work days while they're in school and take night classes."

Mom pulled her hair and screamed loud and long, making so much disturbance my sister came running and crying.

"Delores hates us," Mom screamed louder still. "She's going away."

And that's what happened.

Mom and my sister and brother moved into my grandparents' small home. My grandparents supervised Mom and her topsy-turvy emotions, and she took college classes. She graduated with honors and became a good licensed practical nurse—with greater income and gradually better relationships. She eventually remarried, leaving most of her darkness behind.

In later years, she attended church and made peace with God. She outlived her husband, and we were at her side during the days God prepared her to meet Him. As her cancer progressed, she reached a dreamlike state where she glimpsed her deceased father in a beautiful flower garden with colorful tulips the size of umbrellas.

"Keep watching," I told her. "That's God's flower garden, and He will show you much more."

She nodded, barely conscious.

Sometimes even strong oceangoing ships must fight storms and fierce waves before they reach harbor. I'm thankful God touched Mom's life in ways she could understand. I imagine she's busy helping take care of God's garden.

I'm so thankful that by the end of Mom's life, she, my sister, my brother, and I were all in the best possible place—safe in the arms of Jesus.

I Will Carry You

SANDRA L. HICKMAN

When I grow up, I'm going to be a missionary and go to Africa!

I spoke these words as a little girl. Just the word *Africa* sent shivers of excitement down my spine. The prospect of going there was always in my heart, but who would've thought a little girl from nowhere would ever make it to Africa? Western Australia seemed worlds away from Africa, rendering my dreams impossible.

After what felt like a lifetime, my older daughter, Tari, and I were chosen to be on a missionary team sent by our local church to South Africa for three weeks. That was the original plan, anyway.

Then my pastor called me aside one evening at Bible college and said, "Sandra, I have something to ask you; you'll need to think about this."

"Okay," I responded, wondering what it could be.

"Regarding the mission trip, I've decided to extend it from three to seven weeks. I've accepted an invitation to spend a month in Zambia for a conference. Two of the men from our group will continue on with me, and I'd like you to come as well, for the whole seven weeks, as my intercessor. The rest of the team will return home." He added, "So, as I said, you need to think about it before you make a decision."

Without even a moment's thought I blurted out, "Yes!"

My pastor looked at me. "That was very eager! Are you even going to think about it or pray first?" he exclaimed.

"Oh, well, yes, of course I will think about it and pray about it, but I'm pretty sure my answer will still be yes!" I said.

Tari was happy for me, and I wished she, too, could come for the extra month. However, since she was a single mom with three young children, she could not stretch her time away to seven weeks. My poor parents were aghast at the whole idea. Mom was panic-stricken. "I think it's ridiculous at your age! You're not a young girl anymore, and Africa's a dangerous place."

In my mind I could see my wide-eyed, little-girl self hearing the call of Africa, and in my little-girl heart I was already there. My dad chided, "You'll probably end up in a big pot over a fire like those missionaries you see in the movies!" Oh, my dear Dad could always make me laugh—at least I think he was joking!

So at age fifty-two, I was busy planning a trip to Africa that would last seven life-changing weeks! God took me from wide-eyed little girl to missionary. Even though many years had lapsed in between, it felt like it happened overnight. Who knows but that God will put His calling into the heart of a child and then activate it in His time?

I was bound for Cape Town, Johannesburg, Zambia, and other places. Wow, was I really doing this? After all, I had just jumped in without a life jacket, and my little-girl floaty wings were long gone! So I asked God to confirm that I should go on this seven-week journey. I needed His stamp on it, reassuring my safety. I sought His wisdom and protection.

On the Sunday before we left for Africa, God answered. After an intercessory prayer meeting, a visiting pastor approached me and said, "Ma'am, I have a word for you from the Lord. He says to tell you that He is watching over you. The devil tried to kill you many years ago, and you were supposed to die, but the Lord says, 'It was I who protected you!'"

I could scarcely believe my ears! He continued, "I'm not sure what happened to you; I believe it was an accident. But God says, 'I will look after you.' He gave me this Scripture for you from Isaiah 46:4: 'Even to your old age, I am He, and even to gray hairs I will carry you! I have made, and I will bear; even I will carry, and will deliver you'" (NKJV).

The pastor asked, "Ma'am, do you understand what God is saying?"

Stunned and realizing that God was speaking, I answered, "Yes. Years ago I was in a terrifying car crash with my two young daughters when we hit a huge semitrailer. The front of my car was ripped off and flung through the air, and we flew down into a ditch. The police said the accident should have killed us all. They couldn't believe we had survived, much less completely unscathed!"

The pastor and I stared at each other, knowing this was truly a word from God!

"Well," he said, "I don't know why the Lord is telling me this now, but He wants you to know that *He will* look after you. He has watched you all along, and He will do so even until you are old with gray hairs."

"I've been asking God for confirmation that I should go on a mission trip to Africa. I've been asking Him if I would be safe," I explained. With tears brimming, I added, "My prayer is now answered!"

With the words of this prophet ringing in my ears, I knew God was going to be with me. He would carry me!

A few days later I asked my younger daughter, Bindi, if my granddaughters could come for an overnight stay. The three beautiful little girls, ages one to three, were quite a handful, but I knew how much I would miss them for the next seven weeks. I wanted to have special time with them.

We swapped cars, as Bindi's car had three baby and child safety seats installed. The girls were a joy, but the next morning I awoke with a nasty headache. The thought of driving them home to the farm on the outskirts of town became daunting as the pain in my head increased, gripping me like a skullcap. Nevertheless, I bundled the little girls into their safety seats, and off we went.

I was driving on a lonely country road, feeling dreadful pain, when suddenly, through my driver's side window, I saw a black silhouette of a gangling creature. It was just hovering there as if staring in at me. It was grotesque and had a long body, long, dangling arms, and long, pointed wings; I knew it was demonic.

Just as suddenly, to my utter amazement, a huge shadow of massive wings appeared above the car, spreading over us! I whispered, "Lord, what *is* that?"

I wondered if they were eagle's wings. But they were so huge. As quickly as those big wings appeared, the gangling demon disappeared. And my headache was instantly gone!

It all happened so rapidly. My mind searched for answers. Then my focus turned to the children. I glanced at them, knowing this demon was on assignment, intending to take me out along with the three girls. Immediately I began warfare prayer, covering us in the blood of Jesus, praying all the way to the farm, still awestruck at what had taken place.

I quietly said, "Lord, I will ask you later what those wings were over the car." I was still thinking maybe an eagle's shadow had somehow appeared enlarged by the sun.

As I left the farm, no sooner had I asked, "Lord, what was that over my car?" than He showed me a vision, and I saw *it*! It was not the shadow of an eagle's wings. God showed me an angel whose massive wings spread across the vehicle, protecting me and my three granddaughters. I cried out, "Of course, Lord, of course, it was an angel!" God was showing me that when His angel shows up, demons flee. He protected me, just as the visiting pastor had said He would.

Africa was all I dreamed of and more. God opened my eyes to so many things in the supernatural. I thank God for His Isaiah 46 promise: "I will carry you."

God faithfully carried me for those seven weeks in Africa. Incidents occurred during which I could have been afraid and insecure, or even quite terrified. God reminded me of His promise by telling a godly African sister to bring me another confirming word from Joshua 1:9: "Have I not commanded you? Be strong and of good courage; do not be afraid, nor be dismayed, for the Lord your God is with you wherever you go" (NKJV).

I encountered both good and evil in amazing ways, discovering that when God speaks even the most fearful heart is made bold. He strengthens your spirit to conquer your fearful flesh so nothing can sidetrack you from His plans and promises. His protection is sovereign, and He will carry you.

My Father's Hands

ROBERTA UPDEGRAFF

"Do you want me to go in with you?" my sister asked softly.

I shook my head and pressed my fingertips against the cold steel corridor door. The stench of disease mixed with antiseptics rushed through the crack.

"He's in a coma—probably won't even know you're here." Jen leaned close. "Bobbi, it's not for him. It's for you."

I faked a smile.

"You are the strong one," she reminded me.

I was the one who would not bow under the weight of his failure—his angry tirades against life. I had hooked my future to a star and never looked back.

My sister chose to walk the fence in her relationship with him, hoping for a morsel of praise. Jen and I danced a thousand different versions of sibling rivalry only to end up exhausted—blistered raw by jealousy but always willing to begin again.

The brittle elastic of dysfunction that held us together as siblings had prevented me from pursuing an amiable divorce from my family.

Jen changed the subject. "Dad is the same miserable man. He's probably going to die without ever having to say he's sorry for anything."

Whoever said, "Love means never having to say you're sorry" was dead wrong.

We stood side by side at the door to the ICU. My sister kept her focus on the hallway. The nurses' station was quiet, with one woman perusing a chart. I wanted to say something to Jen—something meaningful, but I'd only make it worse. I took a deep breath. "Might as well bite the bullet."

My sister touched my shoulder and headed back to the waiting area. I closed my eyes and listened to her footfalls. She stopped to talk to the nurse. My sister made it sound as if we were one big happy family.

I took another deep breath and allowed an invisible hand to lead me toward his room. My father looked so small—so old. For a long minute I stood numb, searching my mind for the right greeting.

I took the chair beside him and bowed my head but could not pray.

His right hand was taped with a needle, his fingers were wrinkled, and a yellowish cast to his skin and blue-black protruding veins made his hands look repulsive.

"I'm sorry," I finally whispered, almost against my will.

Then familiar indignation rose from the pit of my belly. In the twenty years since I'd left home, only the victims had changed. I couldn't really blame my youngest brother for beating my father in a drunken rage.

I'd rehearsed a litany of accusations for just this moment, but I sat dumb struck, staring at his hand.

I remembered big, powerful hands, fat hands wrapped around a mug of beer. These were thin—bony, yet there was the same black grease under ragged cuticles, the same half-moon shaped scar on his thumb.

Lub-dub, swish . . . lub-dub, swish, chanted the respirator. Big, scratchy hands held me as I bounced up and down on his knee. "*That lived in the house that Jack built.*" Over and over we had recited my favorite nursery rhyme. He slurred the words, but I didn't care.

I was Daddy's big girl.

In a military hospital in Madrid his finger traced circles on my identification bracelet. He sat by my bed every day until the fever broke.

I was his precious firstborn child.

Lub-dub, lub-dub. Our footsteps exploded in my ears. It was the longest corridor I had ever walked. "There's nothing to be scared of," he said, clasping my hand tightly as we walked to the second-grade classroom in a new town.

I was his little girl.

On my tenth birthday, I watched those shaky hands paint a plaster of paris cat. It was a masterpiece with gray fur and white mittens, just like my cat, Felix. I sat the treasure on my dresser when we returned from visiting him at the hospital.

I was his best girl.

"The Curtin Junior High School award for excellence in history is presented to Roberta Blair."

His clapping resounded in thuds. *Lub-dub, lub-dub*. My mother was in the hospital, having given birth to my youngest sibling days earlier. Dad disappeared right after the ceremony, never mentioning he had been at my junior high graduation, but he framed that certificate.

I was his brilliant daughter.

A loud metronomic *bleep, bleep, bleep* startled me. A nurse rushed in. The curtain brushed my face as they pulled it around my father.

The last thing I saw was his tear-stained finger twitch.

"Is he going to die?" whispered his teenaged attacker when I rejoined my family."God, I didn't mean it," Joey cried.

Jen put her arm around him. "I've wanted to hit him a thousand times."

My sister usually couldn't be in the same room with my father without him spewing criticism. She always laughed it off; I envied that. She could still go to our childhood home, a place I'd avoided for years.

I'd chosen to keep my relationship with my mother, always picking her up and taking her to my house or out somewhere. I made excuses to my children that their grandfather was too sick to visit.

My father's on-again, off-again remorse peppered a lifetime of verbally abusive behavior. A thousand *sorrys* punctuated with *buts* were all he could ever muster. All he had to show for his attempts at recovery was a trail of detox centers, twelve-step programs, and broken promises.

"He had it coming." My sibling closest in age to me rubbed his cigarette into the ashtray. Dan was balding in the same spot as Dad. Gangly arms dangled from the same bony frame. He looked more like my father than the man I'd just left.

"God, I need help." Joey bent his head as if in prayer. "It was the booze—not me."

Jen touched his shoulder. "Shh, it's going to be all right."

Dan lit up another cigarette and rolled it between his fingers. "He's too darn mean to die."

"What happened in there?" my sister asked me.

Dan snickered. "You didn't try to pull the plug, did you?"

I smiled meekly, and Dan laughed—not just a chuckle but a belly chortle that erupted from the painful volcano inside. Dan had taken the most abuse from my father, his physical infirmities a magnet for Dad's terrorizing.

How could I tell them about my experience? I wasn't even sure I wanted to see the better side of my father. "I didn't want to go to jail for murder."

Joey moaned again. "He kept it up—picking and picking. I told him to lay off, but he wouldn't." Joey looked at me. "The first punch was the toughest . . . then I couldn't stop myself. God, forgive me."

"He already has." I smiled, remembering the little boy who had become uncle and playmate to my son.

"Always figured him to be Robo-pop." Dan tapped his finger nervously on the pack of cigarettes. "He'll probably spring up in bed and snarl, 'Gotcha!'"

Well, Robo-pop had his "gotcha." Dad survived the beating, unrepentant. My youngest brother turned his life around and got married. For the next couple of years, I made a haphazard attempt to have a relationship with my father. Perhaps I had a guilty conscience because he wasn't the monster I'd chosen to remember. Most likely it was because of his cancer. They discovered it right after the "incident."

I told everyone at church that I'd forgiven my father and that I'd had a miraculous experience in the intensive care unit that day. They said I was a saint, but my family dismissed me as a religious fanatic. I kept up the appearance of reconciliation and almost fooled myself.

The malignancy spread rapidly to his lungs and finally invaded his brain. I joined a Bible study. I forced myself to pray.

My father bought us all bottles of champagne that Christmas—told us we could toast to his prognosis. That night as I watched my daughter stand beside her daddy, eagerly helping him unwrap a gift, I remembered that day in the hospital and my father's hands. I set my heart on reconciliation and prayed that God would move my father to ask for forgiveness.

When my mother called to tell me his death was imminent, I circled their block three times, praying to forgive my father without conditions. I cried for help to let go of the anger with him and with God for not granting my request.

I wanted him to be sorry for being a terrible father. He wanted me to regret the estrangement I had prescribed.

"It's almost over." His words were barely audible.

I conjured childhood nostalgia to tame the tension. "I do have *some* good memories . . ."

The corners of his lips turned up slightly.

I recalled the Christmas we went tobogganing. We'd traveled from Florida to Pennsylvania to visit his mother. He had steered his childhood sled with my legs wrapped around his waist and my arms hugging him tight.

He reminded me that I had won a prize for an essay I'd written about my first memory of snow.

I closed my eyes and braved necessity. "I imagine how much it has hurt you that I shut you out—"

He raised his hand slightly—stop fashion.

We sat in disquieted silence.

"Dad, you know you've hurt us," I began again.

This time he lifted only a finger.

He turned his head to look at me, eyes brimming with pain.

The silence softened in warm shades of sunset spilling in between the slits in the drawn aluminum blinds.

"You're ashamed, aren't you?" I whispered more to myself than him, as my heart began to comprehend what had held him captive all these years.

"You think you don't deserve compassion—you don't deserve to be forgiven."

Silence wrapped us, as the love we'd denied each other transfused us. All the gnarled, knotted anger drained in my tears, as I held my frail father in my arms.

As dysfunctional as his life had been, he'd given me love. It wasn't the love I expected, but it *had* been enough to sustain me. When I was growing up he'd said I was smart and gutsy, that I could make a difference—and I'd believed him. He may have traded his dreams for booze, but he had given me mine. He'd always wanted to be a writer, and I'd just sold my first essay weeks earlier.

I recited for him my favorite verses from Psalm 139 and shared my discovery that God loves us in spite of our self-loathing. I pointed out that his life had been successful because we were all right—me, my sister, and our four brothers. "We've made good, productive lives for ourselves."

Composure came as naturally as the flood of tears earlier. I recounted the blessings in my life, realizing God was bringing them to mind for strength for this very moment.

My father leaned into my embrace.

"I'll be the best I can be," I whispered, "for you, Daddy."

He squeezed my hand, his grasp warm and firm.

My father died days later.

At the funeral the hospice pastor read the Bible passage Dad had requested in the last moments of his life—Psalm 139.

I wept with joy. One day my father will welcome me home, and he will be the daddy he was always meant to be.

I Got Your Back

CHYNNA LAIRD

I'm not ready to let you go yet.

I've said these words several times in my life. When my grandmother died of Alzheimer's, when my grandfather died after suffering a stroke, when I prayed to save my unborn child, and when I almost lost my Uncle Craig.

My brother, Cam, and I were luckier than most children who grew up the way we did. Our single mother suffered from untreated mental illness and used alcohol, prescriptions, and over-the-counter medications in an attempt to ease her raging mind. Even though we were occasionally thrust into terrible and frightening situations when my mom was manic, we were never completely alone.

We had doting grandparents and an adoring uncle, Uncle Craig, to watch over us in the darkest times. We were blessed more than we realized, considering our circumstances. We never went hungry, we always had a roof over our heads, and most importantly, there was always someone there to offer unconditional love, even when my mom wasn't able to. Without our grandparents and Uncle Craig, Cam and I surely would have gone down a much different and darker path.

Our grandparents were more like our parents, but Uncle Craig, being only fifteen years older than I was, felt more like a big brother than an uncle. He stood up for me, he was there when nobody else was, he brought laughter into my life when I couldn't find it on my own, and he understood what I was going through with my mom. The one thing I valued most about our relationship was the depth of our bond. He always seemed to know when I needed him the most and was there for me without my even having to ask.

After my grandparents passed away, I felt lost. The only people who'd ever been there for me as parents were both gone. But, like always, Uncle Craig was there. We both loved my grandparents dearly and experienced the same torturous loss after each of their passings. I believe in my heart that my grandparents made sure Uncle Craig and I would always be there for one another in their absence.

My earliest memory of our special bond is of one afternoon when Uncle Craig took me to the zoo to cheer me up after a physically confrontational morning with my mother. He took me to see the polar bear exhibit, my favorite animal display back then. He got down on my level, wiped dried blood from my face, then said, "I can't promise you that things will get better or change where you are, but I *can* promise that I'll be here in any way I can. I'll always have your back, kiddo, as I know you'll always have mine."

"Pinky swear," I whispered, holding out my pinky.

He smiled. "Pinky swear."

Then he lifted me up, put me on his shoulders, and pulled my ankles to the sides of his chest. I wrapped my arms around his shoulders and rested my chin on the top of his head. We never said those words out loud again, but as they say, actions speak louder than words. We had each other's back.

I started dreaming about my grandparents after they were both gone. Most of the time it was when I hit a roadblock or low point in my life. And I knew if they were in a dream, there was something in my life I needed to pay attention to. Grandma would come to me whenever my health wasn't where it should have been. Grandpa came to me when I needed a kick in the rear to stay on track. Uncle Craig had the same sorts of dreams. We just figured it was my grandparents' way of reminding us to stay in touch, even when life got busy. And, especially, when we needed each other.

Some would say Uncle Craig and I had a sixth sense about each other. I always said it was God working through us. One of us just knew, or felt, when it was time to reach out to the other. Whether the news was good, bad, or ugly, a phone call was all it would take to say, "Okay, I've heard your voice. I know you're okay. Now I'll be fine." But it was the one and only time I *didn't* respond to one of those feelings that I will never forget.

It happened in 2002. I had barely put in a few months at my prestigious new job with one of the largest law firms in Alberta when I found out I was pregnant. Steve and I were elated, as we'd been trying for almost three years to conceive. Because of health issues, I had to reduce any and all unnecessary stress. That meant I couldn't have contact with my mother's side of my family—except Uncle Craig.

In the beginning of my pregnancy, he called me every week to make sure I was okay and to comfort me with his understanding. He was one of the few people who knew I had health issues that made doctors believe I'd never be able to have children. Obviously, I proved them wrong.

Because of my mother's drinking and her erratic behavior when she drank, I couldn't tell her about the baby. Her instability was something I needed to keep away from my child. Uncle Craig supported my decision and helped me accept that it was okay I hadn't told my mom about the pregnancy. I was doing what I thought was best for my child, and he assured me that if my grandparents were still alive, they'd have said the same thing. The life inside me was more important than anything. "I got your back, kiddo. And now I have a grandniece or grandnephew's back, too!"

Then his calls stopped.

I should have known something was wrong. I guess I convinced myself that if something was truly wrong, someone would let me know. After a month had passed by without word from him, I finally decided to call him. My Auntie Dorothy, his wife, answered.

"Craig hit his head getting out of his car on a business trip a few months ago. He felt fine for a while, but then he started to get severe headaches and dizziness. When he started to experience confusion and speech problems, we took him to the hospital for tests."

Dorothy then told me the doctors said my uncle hit his head in "just the right way" to cause bleeding in his brain. He had to have brain surgery to stop the bleeding and, ultimately, save his life.

I fought back tears. "Why didn't anyone call me? I would have tried to be there for him. For *you*."

"You let me worry about Craig," Dorothy responded wisely. "You have a life inside of you that's depending on you to bring it into the world. You concentrate on *that*. If something happens with Craig, you'll be one of the first to know. You know that."

I knew. But I felt helpless. Uncle Craig had been home for several weeks, but his memory was affected, his speech was poor, and he was going through therapy to remind him how to do the simplest things, like writing. All I could do was pray.

God, please be there for Uncle Craig the way he's always been there for me and for so many other people. Please bring him back to us, even if he's not the same as he was before. Give him the strength he needs to survive and thrive. You brought him into my life to watch over me and to reach out to me. Please remind him to reach out to you now. And let him know I'm here, too. Pinky swear. Always.

I stayed in contact with my aunt and knew if my uncle's condition worsened, she'd tell me. I put everything in God's hands and made myself relax with the thought that I wasn't having dreams about my uncle or urgent gut feelings to contact him. I knew he would be upset if I allowed myself to get so worked up that I lost my child. So I relaxed and continued to pray.

Then, in the last stages of my pregnancy, I received the best phone call ever.

"Hi, kiddo. It's Craig. I just had a feeling I should call and catch up."

A few months later, my first child was born, healthy and safe. It still amazed me how Uncle Craig and I had such an impact on each other, even from a distance. I wasn't ready to let him go at that time, and he wasn't ready to be let go of. Most importantly, the experience made us both realize that our grandparents and God would never let us let go of each other, either.

Sadly, as time passed, and three kids later, I watched my uncle's health worsen. It scared me, but I never let on in our phone calls. The most important gift he gave me, aside from our polar bear visit all of those years ago, was when he came to my wedding in 2015. As he gave me his congratulatory uncle hug, he whispered, "I am so proud of how you've been strong enough to get to this day. Thank you for allowing me to be a part of your life and watch you grow into this incredibly strong woman and mother. And know that no matter what happens after I leave tomorrow, I'll still have your back."

I wasn't quite sure what he meant by that but slowly figured it out. Our phone calls decreased as my life got busier, but I always checked in when the part of my heart I saved just for him—the part that never hardened over no matter how bad things got or who I lost—prompted me. Then the day I feared most of all came.

He passed away. He *left* me. The day I was told is still fresh in my mind. I was getting my children ready for school when my aunt called me. I knew before she said anything. "No," I cried. "Not Uncle Craig."

"I'm so sorry. He went into the hospital and every organ just shut down. I had to be the one to tell you. Please try to get some rest. I'll try calling you later, okay?"

I kept it together until my kids left; then I released every emotion flowing through me until I was exhausted. I had just spoken with him the night before. He gave me no indication that he was that ill. In fact, I had been suffering with health issues, and we talked more about that and my kids than him. Each time I asked, he'd turn the conversation back to his concern for me. It was like part of him knew, and he couldn't tell me . . . or say good-bye.

When I was finally able to fall asleep, I had the most vivid dream. Not only were both of my grandparents there, but my uncle was, too. They were in my grandparents' old living room, sitting in their favorite chairs I remember from childhood.

He finally said good-bye in his way. He held up his pinky and said, "Know, now more than ever, I got your back just as you always had mine."

I hold my kids a bit tighter and longer at good-night time now. I pay more careful attention to my health. And I keep writing, just as they all told me to. Not a day will go by that I won't miss him, or my grandparents. But I will hold my memories close and know that no matter what, someone will always have my back.

Always.

God's Heavenly Army

Barbara Ferguson

I was furious as I left choir practice at the university. Why hadn't I been chosen to sing at the state convention the next week? I was always at choir practice and on time. Not like the spasmodic attendance of some of those who were selected.

As I stomped out the door and began my two-mile trek home, my former boyfriend, Len, saw me and offered a ride. I was upset, and I feared dumping my emotions on him, so I declined his offer and headed out into the cool October night.

Streetlights illumined the sidewalk along Central Avenue. My pity party raged on.

Suddenly a car pulled up beside me and stopped. Leaving the motor running, Len jumped out. "Barbara, let me take you home. God has shown me that you are in danger."

"God doesn't speak to people like that," I said, stomping my foot for emphasis.

He graciously honored my request, returned to his car, and drove away.

A few blocks later I turned down my street, which had very few streetlights. I didn't even see any house lights, and it was only about nine o'clock.

Gradually the vague outline of a man walking toward me emerged from the darkness. I moved to the side to let him pass. As soon as he was behind me, he grabbed me by the throat and threw me over the hedge into a stranger's yard.

I screamed, but nobody seemed to hear. His hands tightened around my neck, so no further sound came out. His heavy body pinned me to the ground, and his fingers began exploring uncomfortable places.

The Holy Spirit reminded me of 1 Corinthians 10:13, which I had memorized: "No temptation has overtaken you except such as is common to man; but God is faithful, who will not allow you to be tempted beyond what you are able, but with the temptation will also make the way of escape, that you may be able to bear it" (NKJV). I knew God provided a ride for me to escape this dangerous experience, but I wasn't listening for His direction, so I ignored the way of escape.

I frantically prayed, "God, forgive my prideful pity party and refusal of the ride you provided. This guy is stronger than me, so there's nothing I can do but rely on you. If you have any plans for the rest of my life, it's up to you."

I completely relaxed in God's loving arms. I saw no heavenly manifestation. But perhaps my attacker saw the heavenly army surrounding him. He released his grip on my throat, jumped up, and bolted down the street as if he'd been shot at.

I gathered my purse and books, which were scattered around the yard, and ran down the street to the first porch light I saw.

A kind lady opened the door and asked if she could help. My incoherent mumbling prompted her to call the police. I heard her tell the operator that she had heard a scream for help. She had turned on the porch light and looked around, listening for further signs of distress. Hearing nothing, she went back into the house but left the porch light on. Now an incoherent young woman who obviously needed help was at her door.

By the time the policeman arrived, I was able to tell him my name, my address, and what had happened. Then he drove me home.

I recounted the ordeal to Mother. Sensing my fear, she stayed in the bathroom while I washed off the dirt from my struggle. At one point she moved quickly, which scared me. I screamed and began shaking violently. It was some time before I was able to go to sleep, so Mother did not wake me up the next morning for my 8:00 a.m. class.

The next day, since we didn't have a car, Mother called a neighbor, explained the situation, and asked if she could borrow her car to take me to the university infirmary. I needed to be examined and receive an excuse for missing my morning classes.

There was no way I would walk by that house with its frightening memories. I had always walked around the town but had never been afraid before. It was a long time before I was able to walk past that house without reliving that terrifying experience. But fortunately, God also reminded me of His supernatural protection and the advantages of memorizing Scripture, listening to Him, obeying Him, and not self-righteously judging or indulging in pity parties.

We got to the campus, and I had some time to spare before my one o'clock class. I went to the noonday devotional service on campus in the building where choir practice had been held the previous evening.

I sat in the front row with my friends. Several boys were behind us. While we stood for prayer, one of the boys evidently leaned on the back of our pew and pushed it slightly forward so it touched the backs of my legs.

I ran screaming out of the chapel. Len was right behind me.

"What happened last night? When I got home, God wouldn't let me get out of the car. He showed me that you were in trouble, so I sat there a couple of hours praying for you."

I described the nightmare and asked for his forgiveness for being so proud, critical, and self-absorbed that I didn't believe him the night before.

He walked with me across campus to my next class. I felt peace as we walked together, but fear consumed me when another person passed close by.

Len helped me make it through. I realized any person this close to God would be a good friend to keep for life.

Len and I began dating again. Eight months later we were married.

God's Promise to a Sixth-Grader

Kay Spivey Walsh

It didn't seem significant the moment it happened. Only in reflection later that day did I recognize God's hand at work. Two seconds. That's all it took. Two seconds to go from chatting with my sister-in-law, Ellie, as we crossed the parking lot to our favorite shop, to lying with my arm and the side of my face plastered on the rough asphalt. I've heard that time stops when a disaster is about to occur, and so it was for me. As I went down, I thought of my knee replacement and that my doctor had said that a fall could be dangerous. I thought of the pain in my other knee . . . of my generous size . . . of how the parking lot slanted down . . .

"Kay! Are you hurt?" cried Ellie.

Thankfully, I didn't feel any broken bones or huge cuts. "I think only my pride was hurt."

Quickly Ellie looked around and said, "Don't worry. I don't see anyone. It's a good thing it's not crowded this morning."

Still dazed, I tried to stand before a car could come around the corner and run me over; however, it became evident this wasn't going to be easy or quick. Even my feet seemed to be tangled, held down by the thick soles of my sneakers. Ellie did her best to help. While I concentrated on turning so I wasn't downhill, I heard a deep voice.

Still contemplating how to best go about this, I heard Ellie ask, "What are we going to do?"

"We're going to pick her up."

"How?"

Without hesitation, his answer came in a calm, confident voice, "Put your hand under her arm. Now, one, two, three . . ."

Wait! Has this man noticed Ellie is a petite woman, probably weighing ninety pounds soaking wet? Has he noticed my size, my age, or that my feet are not in the right position?

They began to lift me so quickly that the only way I could move from this awkward position was to take both feet off the ground at the same time. They didn't seem to notice that, for a few seconds, they carried my entire dead weight. Seamlessly they raised me off the pavement until I could stand. Later, it struck me as odd that I felt equal support on both sides.

Once solidly on my feet, I turned to the man. Again, time stood still. His dark eyes drew mine into his intense gaze. Without wavering, his eyes roamed my face. I felt as though he were reading my soul. Never had a look expressed so much depth and care. A friend, yet someone with authority. Mesmerized, I couldn't look away from his coffee-colored face. While I usually have an abundance of words, I could only squeak out a quiet "Thank you." I noticed a bit of light behind his head, but it didn't register as unusual at the time. He asked if I was okay. I must have said yes because he held my eyes a moment longer, then turned abruptly and walked away. It was only then that I noticed his baseball cap and jeans.

Though a bit shaky, I tried to salvage my pride and act as though the incident was nothing. I brushed my pants and noticed a small cut on my thumb was bleeding. Ellie and I made the usual inane comments that one makes after an embarrassing fall. When we turned to call out our thanks to the man again, he was not in sight, nor was anyone else nearby.

Once I was home, the shock and numbness dissolved and reality hit. The fall could have caused considerable damage, especially if I had hit my head harder or landed on my knees. Ellie and I reflected that the incident seemed surreal. Everything had seemed normal and comfortable, yet a strange feeling lingered. The stranger's piercing eyes still held my thoughts.

Finally, one of us voiced what we both had been wondering: "Do you think we saw an angel?" Our human minds rationalized that it was just a coincidence. We tried to reason away the circumstances. Why would a heavenly body be concerned with us?

Then I remembered an incident from my childhood. Though I had not thought of it in years, it was vividly etched in my mind. I was in the sixth grade. Every school day I caught the first bus, so I rose before anyone else in my family. I found it eerie that the world outside my window was dark and I could hear every creak of the house.

After showering, I would slowly peek out of the bathroom, look up and down the hall, then run to my room. To keep my mind from wandering to scary thoughts, I typically turned on a Christian radio station and sang along. However, this morning there wasn't music but a preacher. He was expounding on his exciting personal visit from an angel. The angel towered over him with huge wings, all white and bright with light surrounding him. The preacher exclaimed what a blessing God had given him, to be in the presence of an angel.

I was terrified. Just the thought of the appearance of an angel left me trembling.

I fell to my knees and pleaded with the Lord to keep me from seeing an angel. I knew God had the power to do anything, including send an angel with a message. Angelic visitations are often mentioned in the Bible, and I recalled that many of the people who saw angels were afraid, even Mary and Joseph and the shepherds in the field. When angels spoke, often their first words were, "Do not be afraid." But I was.

"Lord, I just can't handle it. Don't make me see an angel. Please, not me," I begged.

You will not see an angel until you are ready. You won't be afraid. Angels will appear when you are in need.

As a sixth-grader, I couldn't imagine this future time with peace, yet I felt confident that I had received a promise. Relieved, and still a bit shaky, I continued to prepare for school, but the thoughts of angels lingered.

Now, over forty years later, I knew God's promise to a sixth-grader had come true. Ellie and I had seen an angel in the parking lot, and in his presence there was comfort and love. God had not forgotten His promise to a child who was content with angels who were invisible and silent. That child didn't know yet how much God cared and how He would show himself just as she needed, when she needed, in the way she needed.

The day I fell, I met the God with a "still, small voice," whose magnitude was shown in quiet revelation rather than spectacle. This is the God with whom I can imagine a wonderful eternity.

The funny thing about this is I hadn't envisioned an angel to be a man of average height, with dark eyes, wearing a baseball cap and jeans. And in a parking lot, no less.

Obviously, heaven will be filled with laughter.

Three Precious Young Lives

Susan Guerrero

The blaring ring of the telephone turned out to be the call from hell.

It was a Sunday night. One of my favorite television programs was on—*Touched by an Angel* with Roma Downey.

The inspiring stories portrayed on that program always made me silently congratulate the scriptwriters. The angels and their interactions with humans really had the capacity to touch human hearts every single time the show was aired.

That fateful day, like all days since the births of our son and daughter, began with my asking God to bless and protect both of them. If He sent His angels down to do the job, that was fine, too, as long as the kids were safe and sound in the world.

It was obviously impossible for my husband and me to be with our precious offspring around the clock, so we asked God to take over while they were away from us.

We lived in Tucson, Arizona, at the time. Our then sixteen-year-old daughter was a junior in high school. She was dating a fellow, and they planned to go to the movies that evening.

I said good-bye after reminding her to be sure to make it home before curfew. A pretty girl with dark-brown hair and big brown eyes, she smiled and said she'd be home on time. Then she was off to see a movie with her friend.

She never missed curfew, so I wasn't particularly worried, knowing God and His angels would keep her safe. She always wore a seat belt. Unfortunately, the car was old and made before airbags were mandatory.

It was with joy that I turned on the TV to watch my favorite show. That was something I looked forward to every week, so Sunday nights were kind of sacred. My husband wasn't home when our daughter left for her date, but I expected him back soon.

My program started, and I was comfortably positioned on the couch. Nobody was home to bother me, so I was a happy camper.

Then, hearing the telephone over the voices on the TV, I blurted out, "Oh brother, I'm not answering that."

Honestly, it wasn't appealing to think about getting up from the couch and answering that phone while my show was on, but something nagged at my heart to do it anyway.

Reluctantly, I got up, went to the office, where the landline was located, and picked up the phone. (This was at a time when cell phones were just coming out, and I didn't have one.)

"Hello?" I answered, in a not-too-friendly tone. Pressing the phone to my ear, I could hear sirens in the background.

"Mrs. Susan Guerrero?" the voice on the other end asked.

"Yes, this is she," I managed to say, wanting the caller to hurry up and state her business so I could get back to the program.

"There's been an accident," the unidentified voice said. "Your daughter's car is totaled." She gave the location of the accident, which was just a few blocks from our house.

"Is she okay?" I managed to ask, fear creeping into every fiber of my being.

"The police and medics are here now," the voice said.

"I'll be right there," I said and hung up the phone.

Tears would ordinarily have welled up in my eyes over such news, but not this time. This horrifying event required action, but it was almost impossible to breathe.

"God, my Father, take care of her," was about all I could manage to say, over and over again. "Take care of her, Lord. Take care of our precious daughter."

With my hand shaking uncontrollably, I managed to dial my husband's cell phone. By the grace of God, he answered.

"Honey, Gabriela has been in an accident," I remember saying.

"Where?" his voice replied.

"Right near our house," I said. "Please, come pick me up so we can go there."

He said he'd head straight home and was there in a very short time.

I slid into the passenger's seat, and the two of us drove in the direction of the accident scene. From a couple of blocks away, we could see lights flashing. There were police cars, ambulances, and firefighters.

My heart was racing so fast that I thought it was going to jump out of my chest. The whole scene seemed surreal. Still struggling to breathe, I kept my eyes on the flashing lights in the distance, talking to God all the way over.

When we got closer, my husband pulled the car over to the side of the road. Traffic was blocked off from the crash.

We gasped when we saw the pile of mangled metal that used to be our daughter's car. Part of it was wrapped around a utility pole. The rest was smashed like a sardine can.

The windshield had a gaping hole in it, surrounded by smashed glass. Her head had hit and gone through the windshield.

"Dear God," I whispered as I clasped my hand into my husband's. "Oh God, help her."

Then the tears came. They poured out without control as I tried to get to my daughter's car. The jaws of life were working on getting her out. I lifted my arm up to wipe away the tears that were blinding me. Swipe, swipe, swipe. The more I wiped, the more the tears poured out.

I squinted my eyes as much as possible to try to see her inside the car as we hurried toward it, but the police stopped us.

"Hold it right there," an officer said. I felt strong hands on both shoulders, stopping me from moving.

"But that's our daughter," my husband blurted out.

"They are doing everything possible to help her," the policeman told us. "The ambulances are ready to take them to the hospital."

"Them?" I questioned. Of course, her boyfriend was there, too. His parents lived in Wisconsin and would be distraught to know this was happening. Was he alive? Was our daughter alive? Would there be lifelong injuries with which to contend? Would they ever be able to see again? Walk? Be regular teenagers who go to proms, look forward to high school graduation, and apply to colleges?

Thoughts in my mind were whirling together like liquid in a blender on high speed. Through it all, I kept trying to take a deep breath, but somehow my lungs would not fill with air. Little puffs of breath were all I could manage.

There is nothing on earth more frightening for a parent than to contemplate losing a child. No matter the age, that child is precious to the mother who gave her life. A father, too, knows that child is his precious baby who is growing up. She is part of a parent's very heart and soul.

The sirens and noises of machines filled the warm night air as the extrication from the car continued.

Apparently, another car had crashed into our daughter's, propelling it into a huge utility pole. To this day, I do not remember seeing the other car or its young male driver, who had drunk a dozen beers before slipping behind the wheel. It wasn't even his car. It belonged to a family member of his. That is what we found out weeks after the accident.

At last, we saw ambulance attendants wheeling a stretcher to the side of our daughter's car. A policeman came over and told us what hospital she and her boyfriend were going to be transported to.

I tried to move toward the stretcher to hold her hand, but the police wouldn't let me go.

"We're here, honey," I yelled out as loud as I could. "Poppy and I are here. We are going to follow you to the hospital, Gabriela. You are going to be okay."

I have no idea whether she heard me. Total strangers were putting their arms around me as heavy weeping heaved through my body.

"God, help her, please," I stammered through sobs. "God, my Father, help her, please."

My husband finally grabbed my hand and told me we had to go back to our car and drive to the hospital.

It was a long, torturous drive along a road lined with houses and streetlights. Looking out the car window through a veil of tears, I wondered why all this was happening. How could our precious daughter's life be hanging in the balance, as well as the life of her boyfriend? It still didn't seem like it was really happening, but it was.

Once at the hospital, we parked our car and ran in. The ambulances had already arrived, and our daughter and her boyfriend were inside, being tended to by doctors and nurses. My husband and I weren't allowed to go into the treatment area with them. We huddled together in a waiting room, holding each other while we both cried and prayed.

After what seemed like an eternity, a nurse came out and asked if we were Gabriela's parents. We nodded, holding our breath and finally standing on shaky legs.

"You can see her now," the nurse said.

She was in an emergency room bed, covered with white sheets up to her neck. When we walked in, she looked right at us with those big, beautiful brown eyes of hers.

"Hi," she said, in a soft, chipper voice.

"Are you okay, honey?" I asked, going to the side of the bed. She took her arms out from beneath the sheets, and I gently held one of her hands.

At the time of impact, the dashboard of her car collapsed on her legs. Miraculously, she had just a few bumps, scrapes, and cuts.

Despite the fact that her head had gone through the windshield, she was alert and cognizant.

A doctor came in and said our daughter had somehow escaped serious injury. He felt that with therapy and rest, she would definitely be able to walk again.

Right then and there, I knew how and why she had lived. It truly was a miracle of huge proportion. Almighty God and His angels had saved her young life. What could have been a total tragedy turned out so differently.

If our daughter had not been wearing her seat belt, she probably would have been thrown from the vehicle. But if the car had been made with airbags, she would not have gone through the windshield. With God's help, she survived it all.

Her boyfriend was banged up but escaped serious injury. We were able to reach his parents by phone later that evening and fill them in on what had happened.

The driver of the car that plowed into our daughter's car had definitely been drunk. He, too, escaped serious injury and was arrested and charged.

After several months, court hearings, and pleas from Mothers Against Drunk Driving, he was eventually sentenced to two years in jail for drunk driving with bodily injury.

Our daughter required many months of physical therapy for her legs, which many years later still occasionally give her problems.

She has migraines, too, but she handles them with medication.

She is the mother of three beautiful children, a little girl and twin toddler boys.

The boyfriend who was in the accident with her is long gone, living his own life in his home state.

I don't know what became of the drunk driver, but with all my heart I hope he learned a valuable lesson from that night.

We never learned who called our house the night of the accident or how she got our phone number.

My husband and I definitely believe the Lord saved three young lives that night. Whenever we drove past the utility pole after that, the thoughts and feelings kicked up again, bringing fresh pain but also relief and gratitude.

We moved away from Arizona, back to the East Coast, and for the rest of our lives we will remain ever grateful to God for sparing our daughter's life. We are deeply grateful, too, to the Tucson police, firefighters, and medical personnel who attended to her the night of the accident. They were all earthly angels.

To the heavenly angels who were there, too, goes our heartfelt gratitude. Whenever I see reruns of *Touched by an Angel*, I am reminded that angels really do exist and miracles still happen.

For God and His angels and the miracle of three young people escaping death in that horrible accident, I will remain deeply grateful for the rest of my days on earth.

The Gossamer Curtain

Ruth Smith Meyer

My husband, Norman, and I married young. We were in love. But we had our ups and downs. At the ten-year mark of our marriage, we went through a crisis. In the next ten years we struggled valiantly to come back from the brink of divorce. Through a Marriage Encounter event, we finally learned to truly listen to each other and accept each other as we were. Happily, we found love deeper than we ever thought it could be. Life was so different and beautiful.

Having thirty-eight years behind us and looking forward to truly living and serving as a team, we were blindsided in March when Norman was diagnosed with colon cancer. Through the next seven months we went forward with hope, expecting to come out the other side just as we had with other challenges in our lives.

The first surgery to remove part of his colon seemed to be successful, but in June the doctors thought removing a lobe of his liver where they had discovered a spot would give him a better chance of survival. That halted the progress he had been making. He was unable to sleep. The lack of adequate rest broke down his body's ability to fight, and he went into a sharp decline. Through this, we continued to deeply share our feelings, our fears, and our delights.

In August, our journey started to have an otherworldly feel to it. I began to have vivid dreams of us walking together toward a bridge. When we'd near the bridge, an angel would hold me back and let me know that Norman needed to walk alone over that crossing. At other times, we'd walk through a beautiful garden. After a while, we'd come to a gate where the colors on the other side were more brilliant than anything I've ever seen. We would pause on this side of the gate. I knew I couldn't go through, but that he would. I always woke up just as we were sharing a good-bye hug.

In September, we celebrated thirty-nine years of marriage, but Norman was a shadow of the man I married. A few weeks later, at a visit to our doctor, Norman asked how long he might have. He was told, "Perhaps two weeks."

On the way home, I asked Norman how he felt about that. He said, "Ruth, I know it won't feel this way to you, but to me it is a relief."

I paused to let my mind and heart settle a bit. "Norman, I have tried throughout our marriage, and especially in this past year, to help you live well. If the time has come to let you go, I will try just as hard to help you die well."

Tears came to his eyes as he squeezed my hand.

In the days following, we were at ease and yet felt on the verge of dramatic change. Norman often voiced assurance that I could make it on my own and that he had confidence in me. He spoke of his feelings—the anticipation of leaving the pain of this world, but also some uneasiness because he didn't know how it would feel when the moment of death came.

In October, two days before his death, he was no longer able to manage the few steps to our living and dining room, so we had our meals in the office just across the hall from our bedroom. As I was helping him eat, he asked, "Who else is here?"

"There's no one else here, Norman. We're alone—just the two of us."

"No." He shook his head. "There's someone else here."

"I don't think so. Just you and me."

"I think perhaps it's the angels," he surmised.

Realization dawned on me. "Well, if they came for you, Norman, you can go when you are ready," I assured. That seemed to satisfy him.

The next night, his breathing was very shallow. We put a CD of his beloved Handel's *Messiah* on. When it came to the "Hallelujah Chorus," his toes moved in time to the music. We thought the "Amen Chorus" was going to usher him into eternity, but when it was finished, he was still with us. I sent his sister and our daughter to bed and crawled into our queen-sized bed with him. He reached for my hand and squeezed it.

"I didn't think I'd still be here," he whispered.

"I guess your time isn't quite here yet."

I told him again how much I loved him and what a good husband he'd been—how glad I was for the depth of our relationship and love. He also expressed his love and thankfulness for what I meant to him. We fell asleep.

At 4:30 a.m., I was awakened by Norman's voice joyfully saying, "Yes, yes, yes!" When I turned on the bed lamp, his eyes were shining like a little child's at Christmastime. He couldn't say much more, but occasionally he would joyfully say again, "Yes!"

It seemed as though he could hardly wait to move forward to what he was seeing.

The sun was almost up when he whispered with a satisfied sigh, "Home!" With each breath, he whispered it again. There was such gratification and contentment in his voice—pure fulfillment and joyful consummation. Even though he was still breathing, I felt his spirit leave his body and fill the whole room.

I laid my head on the pillow beside him and sang, "Lead me gently home, Father, lead me gently home." I sang the song through twice. Just as I finished the second time, the sun rose and shone in our eastern picture window by the bed. His breathing stopped, but his spirit still filled the room.

I felt a little like I did when I rocked and sang my children to sleep then laid them down on their beds. I still sang a bit longer to make sure they were fully asleep. I had sung my husband into eternity, but I waited in his presence and in the presence of the divine. The beauty of the moment overwhelmed me, and I cried out in joy, "Thank you, thank you, Lord!"

The gossamer curtain between this earth and the next world was so thin at that instant. I could scarcely believe the holy presence I felt, the privilege of standing so close to the other side. I lingered until I felt the fullness of his spirit slowly leave. It felt as if it rose and slowly swept out the window and upward.

In the stillness and peace, I marveled. It was difficult to fathom. That moment such a great part of me had departed, but it also provided me a revelation. Time and eternity were not nearly as far apart as I had believed. It changed my outlook on life forever.

About the Contributors

Rose Alexander serves her Savior through writing from her home in Ohio.

Jan Apilado has recently found a new purpose in encouraging widows, as she has lost her beloved husband, Corky. She is also a prayer warrior and women's speaker who lives in the Cascade Mountains.

Dee Aspin is the author of two devotional books, *Lord of the Ringless* and *Dogspirations*. Dee enjoys writing human- and animal-interest stories. She has works published by CBN, Barbour, Revell, *Guideposts*, and more.

Paul F. Bauer is a retired police lieutenant, a licensed professional counselor, and the author of *40 Days in the Desert: A Devotional Guide for Uniform Services Personnel*.

Carolyn Roth Barnum coordinates "Write People" at Wesley Village, Wilmore, Kentucky. Her stories have appeared in Grace Publishing anthologies, *Woman's World*, and *Reminisce* magazine.

Laurie Allred Boyd was born in 1960, and she is a facilitator of success who writes with the goal of empowering others to grow in their relationship with Christ.

Wanda J. Burnside is a teacher, the author of sixteen books, a poet, and the publisher of the *Lamp Newsletter*. She has been married since 1972 to Simmie Lee Burnside, Jr.

Sharon Padgett Campbell and her husband of fifty-six years live in a retirement community. She enjoys scrapbooking, making jewelry, and singing in a choir. She has two children and five grandchildren.

Ronald C. Daniel is a retired hospice chaplain in Georgia who graduated from Luther Rice College & Seminary with a degree in biblical counseling and religion.

Midge DeSart is a church musician and the author of a women's Bible study, *Maintaining Balance in a Stress-Filled World*.

Barbara Ferguson's experience so influenced her life as a young Christian that she has had a passion to know God better and share Him with others for over sixty years.

Elizabeth Garrett established Polish Point Editing in 2016 to provide author coaching and editing services. Her creative works, both fiction and nonfiction, have been published in numerous publications.

Susan Guerrero has been writing for most of her life. She has a journalism degree. She has written more than 2,700 posts for her blog, *Writing Straight from the Heart*.

Caryl Harvey is a writer and amateur living-history interpreter. She and her husband were foster parents for sixteen years and adopted three children and have four biological children.

Melissa Henderson and her husband, Alan, live in the Low Country of South Carolina. Melissa enjoys writing, reading, and volunteering. Visit her blog at www.melissaghenderson.com.

Judith Victoria Hensley is a retired middle school teacher, weekly newspaper columnist, photographer, blogger, and speaker. She has authored Appalachian folklore, middle school chapter books, and Christian fiction.

Sandra L. Hickman is an Australian Christian author, poet, and songwriter. She is also a missionary, having served in Africa, India, and China, and is the Australian ministry leader for the *Lamp Newsletter* in Detroit, Michigan.

Sharilynn Hunt teaches others about prayer through New Creation Realities Ministry, www.ncrministry.com. She has published stories in numerous anthologies, including *Chicken Soup for the Soul: Best Mom Ever!* and *Life-Changing Miracles*.

Chynna Laird writes from her home in Edmonton, Alberta, Canada.

Ruth Smith Meyer enjoys observing life as she continues to learn and mature. Widowed twice, she shares the understanding and growth with which she has been gifted.

Craig Nelson works for Scheels and enjoys taking in Husker football games.

Peggy Park has three published books: *The Power of the Lamb's Blood*, *Unshackled*, and *Grandmother's Journal*. Her writing credits include articles for various Christian magazines.

Hailing from Tucson, Arizona, **Alyssa Roat** is a freelance writer and a professional writing major at Taylor University.

Fran Sandin is a retired registered nurse, organist, grandmother, and author, who enjoys community Bible study and traveling with her husband, hiking, and flower arranging. Visit her website at www.fransandin.com.

Ingrid Shelton is a retired teacher and librarian. She has had numerous stories and articles published in the CHICKEN SOUP FOR THE SOUL series and *Guideposts*. She loves gardening, walking, reading, and sharing the Good News.

C. F. Sherrow lives in the Denver area. She practiced medicine as a physician assistant for twenty-three years and is now a counselor and writer. Her first novel, *Dark Heritage*, was released in 2017.

E. V. Sparrow writes from her home in Rocklin, California.

Kelly J. Stigliano has been a speaker and writer for over thirty years. She and her husband, Jerry, enjoy life in Orange Park, Florida. To learn more, please visit www.kellystigliano.com.

Ronica Stromberg is the author of four children's books and writes for various Christian magazines.

Steven Thompson is the father of four adult children and a grandfather of five. He freelances from his home in northern Iowa.

Delores E. Topliff lives near Minneapolis. She loves Jesus, family, grandchildren, friends, mission trips, travel, and her small farm. She also enjoys writing and teaching college courses.

Roberta Updegraff is an author with *Guideposts*. She enjoys volunteering in a Honduran orphanage, traveling, reading, quilting, and researching genealogy.

Judith Vander Wege wants to help hurting people get into an intimate relationship with God and experience His love and healing. She and her husband attend a First Reformed church.

Elfriede Volk and her husband have traveled the world as volunteer missionaries and evangelists since 1977. Last year their daughter Karen joined them, preaching her first evangelistic series in Kenya.

Kay Spivey Walsh lives in the Shenandoah Valley of Virginia with her husband, a horse, and a dog. She teaches at James Madison University and leads the Shenandoah Christian Writers group.

Susan M. Watkins, award-winning author, wrote for *The 700 Club* television program. She is featured in multiple publications and on CBN.com. She has also written for bestselling author Max Lucado.

Barbara Wells is a published author, international speaker, radio personality, and member of AWSA (Advanced Writers and Speakers Association). For more information, visit www.barbarawells.webs.com and www.facebook.com/barbarawellsauthor.

Martin Ziegner has been a general dentist for over forty years in the western suburbs of Chicago. He has two adult children, three dachshunds, and a parrot.

James Stuart Bell is a Christian publishing veteran and the owner of Whitestone Communications, a literary development agency. He is the editor of many story collections, including *Angels, Miracles, and Heavenly Encounters*; *Jesus Talked to Me Today*; and *Gifts From Heaven*, as well as the coauthor of numerous books in the COMPLETE IDIOT'S GUIDE series. He has cover credit on more than one hundred books, and he and his wife live in a western suburb of Chicago.

More from James Stuart Bell

These extraordinary true stories of miracles, healing, and encounters with angels and demons will boost your faith through evidence of God's continuing involvement in our world.

Heaven Touching Earth

These inspiring true stories of heavenly victories over difficult circumstances and opposing forces will strengthen your faith and leave you astounded. You will marvel at how God and His angels are working behind the scenes to protect and guide us.

Angels, Miracles, and Heavenly Encounters

You May Also Like . . .

In this remarkable story collection, ordinary people just like you recount miraculous and astounding answers to prayer. This book will strengthen your faith and inspire you to believe that God can and does answer our most seemingly impossible prayers, fulfilling our deepest needs and biggest dreams in ways we could never imagine.

Gifts from Heaven

Children have a special place in Jesus' heart and His kingdom. This touching collection of true stories shows how God works in the lives of little children, whose hearts are so open to encountering God. We could all use more childlike faith, and these stories—from the mouths of babes—will inspire you to be open to hearing from the Lord in a fresh, pure way.

Jesus Talked to Me Today

BETHANYHOUSE